Typewriter Art

Edited and with a introduction by Alan Riddell

London Magazine Editions

By the same author
The Stopped Landscape (poems)
Eclipse (concrete poems)

Copyright © 1975 London Magazine Editions

Published by London Magazine Editions
30 Thurloe Place, London SW7

Designed by Ron Costley and printed in England by Shenval

ISBN 900626 99 2

End-papers: Chromatic permutations by Luigi Ferro (1967)

This book is to be returned on or before
the last date stamped below.

(*For description see*)
(*previous page.*)

Drawing of a butterfly made in England by Flora F. F. Stacey in 1898. It is the earliest dated example of a typewriter art work for Ann

Contents

To fit the format of the book, some works have had to be
slightly enlarged or reduced

List of plates

The image in the machine

An American, Christopher Latham Sholes, is widely held to be the inventor of the first practical typewriter. His machine, perfected in the early 1870s, was bought by E. Remington & Sons, gunsmiths, of Ilion, New York, and put on the market in 1874.

Mark Twain wrote to his brother in 1878 of this 'new-fangled writing machine': 'It will print faster than I can write. One may lean back in his chair and work it. It piles an awful stack of words on one page. It don't muss things or scatter ink blots around. Of course it saves paper.'

In the century since then, the typewriter has become so much a part of life that it is hard to imagine our present society without it. More than taking the drudgery from writing, it has transformed business and created the largest female workforce in history, the monstrous regiment of typists.

The typewriter's role as an artistic instrument is less familiar. In choosing these 119 works by 65 practitioners from 18 countries, I have tried above all to pay tribute to the machine itself, and its particular qualities. Thus the images are not arranged by author, by country or chronologically, but mainly in juxtapositions to show the range of effects possible with the typewriter. For example, Simon Parritt's 'Grid 4' and Andrew Belsey's 'Train types', on facing pages 62 and 63, both use the same building block – two horizontal and two oblique strokes: $\square$ – but to quite different purpose. And the nine heads grouped together on pages 66 to 74 illustrate the varied possibilities in figuration, from the almost photographic realism of Will Hollis's Arab to the stylised study of the artist's wife by the Jugoslav Zoran Popović.

Where the appearance of an image has not determined the choice of the next, the theme may be the link, as with Helmut Zenker's 'Sunday' and Bob Cobbing's 'Whisper Piece' on pages 146 and 147.

In general, figurative works predominate in the earlier part of the book and abstract and geometric ones towards the end. I have departed from this arrangement, however, in the opening pages, which are devoted to three pioneers of the 1920s – Hendrik Nicolaas Werkman, Pietro de Saga and an unidentified Bauhaus student of Josef Albers' – whose works give an historical context to the profusion of present-day experiment.

Although these three showed how the typewriter could be used to produce imaginative art, people had been experimenting on the machine since it came on the market. In Britain, the typewriter in its early days seems to have been regarded with the same blend of idealism and hard-sell that attached to the computer in the 1960s. Propagandists claimed that it would benefit not only business but also education (by improving spelling and punctuation) and the emancipation of women (J. M. Barrie wrote a play, 'The Twelve-Pound Look', in 1910 about the independence being able to type gave to women).

In the 1890s, typewriter manufacturers and secretarial agencies organised public speed-typing competitions, and also competitions for typewriter drawings. The latter seem to have been popular with typists – or type writers, as they were then called – though our frontispiece, composed by Miss Flora F. F. Stacey in 1898, is one of the few examples to have survived. Pitman's Phonetic Journal, which printed it, commented:

'We think it will be generally admitted that the illustration is in the highest degree creditable to the artistic ability, skill and patience of the lady, and to the unique capabilities of the Bar-Lock for this class of work. It may be noted that in competitions for typewriter drawings Miss Stacey has been extremely successful. . . . An outsider, or one unaccustomed to the use of the typewriter, can scarcely realise what an expenditure of time and patience is necessary in order to successfully execute one of these curious drawings. The paper has, of course, to be turned and re-turned, and twisted in a thousand different directions, and each character and letter must strike precisely in the right spot. Often, just as some particular sketch is on the point of completion, a trifling miscalculation, or the accidental depression of the wrong key, will totally ruin it, and the whole thing has to be done over again.'

It would be hard to better this description of one approach to typewriter composition. However, if the decorative border of Miss Stacey's work is discounted, one sees its basic weakness. With the exception of the letter o, the keyboard's alphabetical characters are not used: the drawing is composed of brackets, hyphens, points, oblique strokes and a single asterisk. They make up a sketch of a butterfly which could just as well, and far more easily, have been done with pen and ink, and one which denies rather than affirms the instrument with which it was made.

H. N. Werkman's 'typeprints', by contrast, illustrate how a gifted artist sets out to exploit a medium. Werkman, who was born in 1882 in Leens in the Dutch province of Groningen, began his working life as a journalist. He later moved into printing, first as manager of a comparatively big firm and then, after the economic collapse following the First World War, as a small jobbing printer. He had already begun to paint in oils during the war but now found a new way to express his creativity. The jobbing printer must personally master the related skills of typography and layout, typesetting, composing (the insertion of the type into the iron chases in which it will be printed), and the printing itself. These came easily to Werkman, and he went on to become a typographer of originality and a maker of intuitively structured prints using the stock-in-trade of the printing shop – large display types, rules, inking rollers, even the rectangular mounts of the letters themselves. His work in both these areas has been increasingly recognised. Werkman's typewriter experiments also date from this time – 1923 to 1929 – but it is only now, fifty years later, that these are coming to be fully appreciated (pages 19 to 26).

Werkman uses the rectilinear grid of the typewriter as a framework against which to explore the abstract visual rhythms of the keyboard's signs and letters. Two of his techniques are worth pointing out. For any given typeprint he generally allows himself two insertions of the paper, one at right angles to the other; and he disengages the typewriter's line-spacing mechanism and moves the paper up or down as required to get unstraight lines. By the first of these devices he produces elaborate patterns of crosshatching, and by the second a delicate interplay between the straight and wavering lines. One is reminded of electrical circuit diagrams and the contour lines on maps.

At the same time as Werkman was experimenting in northern Holland, Josef Albers in Germany was using the typewriter as an artistic tool in his preliminary course at the Bauhaus in Dessau. The works reproduced here were done under his tutelage and were exhibited at the big Bauhaus show at the Royal Academy in London in 1968. Unfortunately, neither Professor Albers nor the Württembergischer Kunstverein, which organised the show, have been able to trace them since then and so only enlarged half-tone illustrations taken from the exhibition catalogue are now available. This accounts for the furriness of the straight lines and the breaking up of the letters and other signs. However, the originality of these 'construction exercises', as Albers called them, is immediately apparent, notably in the stylish way in which a three-dimensional image is created. In two cases this comes from the use of horizontal and oblique strokes (on page 29 the closely-packed diagonal lines also give added weight of tone and the effect of shading to the geometrical form). In the other instance (page 28), three-dimensionality is created by one plane cutting through another. (Horizontal and oblique strokes also form the basic technique by which Dom Sylvester Houédard produces his three-dimensional effects.)

Little is known about the third member of this pioneering trio, Pietro de Saga, beyond the fact that this was the pseudonym of Stefi Kiesler, wife of the Austrian architect Friedrich Kiesler, who in the 1920s published typewriter work in the Bauhaus magazine when it was edited by Walter Gropius. She later emigrated to the United States, where she is believed to have died.

The 1930s were a dead decade for typewriter art, but by the end of the Second World War the Pole Stefan Themerson, who had settled in London, was publishing his 'semantic divertissements', which wittily combined typewriting used in a visual way with illustrations by his wife Franciszka, the painter. But these were mixed-media experiments; his contribution here, done in 1946, is purely a typewriter work and forms the bridge between the pioneers of the 1920s and the present generation of practitioners. Although Themerson uses a text (page 103), and so looks forward to later typewriter experiments by the concrete poets, it is easy to imagine his approach finding favour in both Groningen and Dessau.

The international concrete poetry movement of the 1950s and 1960s gave a new impetus to typewriter experiment, and also added a new element to it: semantic content. Poems combining the verbal with the visual were composed on the typewriter in increasing numbers. Some of these concrete poems could be realised in print or – later, when it was invented – with transfer lettering such as Letraset. But others, because of the difference between typesetting and typing, are difficult, or impossible, to realise in print. For instance, to superimpose one line on another in printing requires two separate lines of type to be set, two separate formes to be composed, and finally two separate printings – a costly operation. With the typewriter one simply pushes the carriage back to the beginning of the line, or uses the back-spacer, and starts typing again (figure 1).

Another distinction between printing and typewriting is that the print letters vary in width, an m or a w being much wider than an l, whereas the typewriter's characters are all the same width. This means that a typed text in which successive lines are

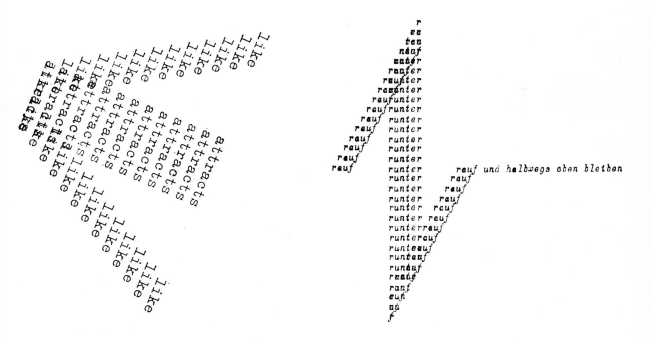

```
lesbares in unlesbares übersetzen
      lesbares in übersbares
            lübbarbären
              übarbären
```

reduced in length by one letter will have a straight diagonal outline, as in the Stefan Themerson work. In print, the diagonal outline would come out irregular and the crisp geometry of the design would be lost. Several concrete poets have suffered from misguided attempts to translate their typewriter works into normal print (though a few printers do have a special 'typewriter' typeface with the letters all the same width).

Paradoxically, this distinction of the letter widths no longer exists with some advanced typewriters which were developed as an alternative to typesetting when printing labour costs rose in the 1960s. These 'near print' machines have keyboards which give the same spacing and appearance as conventional type. Books produced by this method are characterised by ragged margins on the right. Many typewriter concrete poems cannot be typed on 'near print' typewriters.

Figure 2 Emmett Williams' typewriter concrete poem is more eye-catching than the Claus Bremer one at the top of the page. However, although it projects a verbal statement in a visual dimension, it remains only a border-line case of typewriter art

Figure 3 Another example, by Reinhard Döhl, of a borderline case of typewriter art ('Up down up and staying halfway up'). For a typewriter concrete poem which is also clearly typewriter art, see Timm Ulrichs' 'Condensation' on page 81. Constructed on the same principles as these three concrete poems, it is visually much more interesting

Not all typewriter concrete poems can be called typewriter art. Only those which explore the instrument's visual possibilities interestingly are considered so here, and many otherwise excellent poems have had to be left out of the body of this book. Figure I is an example of typewriter poetry which is not typewriter art. Figures 2 and 3 are borderline cases in which the visual element is stronger than in figure I, though not yet as strong as in Timm Ulrichs' similarly structured but more visually dynamic 'Condensation' (page 81). Some works coexist elegantly in both genres: for example, Paula Claire's 'Sea shanty' (page 59) and Jiří Kolář's 'Fountain' (page 35) are as good concrete poems as they are typewriter art.

In other works of typewriter art, the letters used bear no intelligible relationship to the image, as in Jeremy Adler's 'Leaflikebird' (page 33), a graceful abstraction of movement in which subtle differences of tone and texture are produced by typing rows of a's on a sheet of paper rotated by small degrees through 130 degrees.

Understandably enough, pattern-making is popular (Ferro, Nannucci, Etlinger), and the typewriter has had its op artists (Ulrichs, Valoch, Kostelanetz). In fact, looking over these works one sees that many recent art movements have been reproduced on the typewriter. Constructivist and systems art, op and gestural abstraction have all been typed, and sometimes not only under the influence of other media – Ulrichs' op effects (page 119) were being produced in the very early 1960s at the same time as Bridget Riley's.

There might appear to be a similarity between typewriter works and computer graphics, but they are not really alike. The typewriter artist makes one mark on the paper by depressing a chosen key once, and a succession of such choices – often an infinitely laborious process – is required to finish the design. The computer artist feeds his mathematical programme into the computer, which transforms it in a matter of minutes into mind-bending curves and forms. His skill comes in the programming, and in the selecting of the images produced – computers can make elaborate and appealing designs when programmed in error or when set to operate at random.

A medium closer to the typewriter is the teleprinter, and I have included one example: an illustration from Willard S. Bain's teleprinter novel, *Informed Sources*.

One traditional craft has a similarity to typewriter work: embroidery on canvas. This has a rectilinear grid on which the design is built up one stitch at a time. And where the embroiderer uses different coloured thread to produce light and shade and shape, the typewriter artist as a rule does so by choosing letters of varying densities.

Coloured typewriter ribbons and coloured carbon paper can, of course, be used, though many practitioners prefer ordinary black ribbon – and black and white is more readily accepted for publication. Nevertheless, when colour is used well it can add greatly to the expressiveness of a typewriter work, as in Tom Edmonds' 'Towards me writing a book' (page 104), completed not long before he died in 1971 at the early age of twenty-seven. This was typed with red and black ribbon and blue and black carbon paper. Luigi Ferro offers another ingenious colour effect by typing with red and black ribbon on to transparent paper and then inserting an orange-coloured paper behind this. The result is a three-colour composition achieved by the simplest means. Typewriter images can also be reproduced in colour by silk-screen printing or by the traditional colour-printing methods used in book-production: as in 'Aubade' on page 111. These give almost unlimited colour possibilities.

So far as I can see, the late Will Hollis achieved most of his colour effects by tinting black and white works, as photographers did before the introduction of colour film. But his skill in separating a photographic image into its constituent tonal values, matching these to the weight of different typewriter characters and then reconstituting the image on the typewriter is truly remarkable (pages 65 and 66).

His method must have been very much the same as that used by Dennis Collins in making his portraits of the Queen, the Duke of Edinburgh and Churchill, and described in a letter to me:

'What started me on these was when I was with an advertising agency. My employer always had a prime-position page ad. on the inside front cover of *Advertisers Annual* and one year I had the idea of taking a small thumbnail photo of him, from which I had a coarse half-tone block made, and then having a proof of this blown up to the full-page size. At first glance this was rather a puzzle with the very large half-tone dots, but was clearly his face when held at arm's length. This set me thinking of the tone values of typewriter characters, and I made a graduated scale of tones, from the lightest (a full stop) to the darkest (s over w). I then used this scale to translate the tones of a photograph.

'The Queen's portrait and the Churchill one were done on an old portable on which spaces could not be finely adjusted – this accounts for the horizontal white strips across the faces. . . . The Duke of Edinburgh one was done when I lashed out and bought an Olivetti.'

Some other techniques may be worth pointing out: using masking paper or 'whiting out' with paint to produce an outline; overprinting images through duplicating stencils; using carbons to get blurred or smudged effects.

There are, of course, limitations to the typewriter as an artistic medium. An obvious one is the narrowness of the paper the machine can accommodate. But this can be overcome by planning a large design in panels and typing these separately. Steve McCaffery has produced by this method a 34-by-44-inch composition in black and red using sixteen separate sheets (two contiguous panels are reproduced on pages 108 and 109).

In fact, much of the pleasure of typewriter art lies in the way in which individual practitioners have overcome the technical problems.

But more than this: by welcoming a technological commonplace like the typewriter, the contributors to this book show how technology and art can continue to reinforce each other. Indeed, many of the most exciting works here are among the most recent – notably those composed in the 1970s by Tom Edmonds, Steve McCaffery and Dom Sylvester Houédard.

Alan Riddell

Pioneers

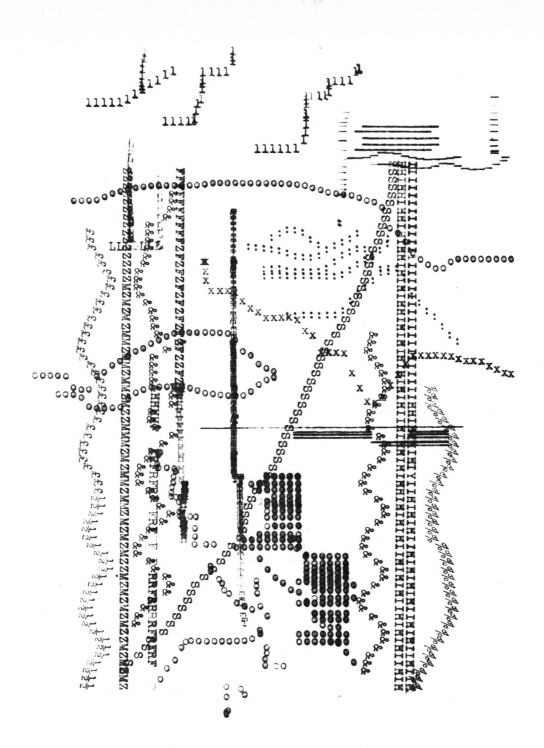

Typeprint H. N. Werkman (1923–29)

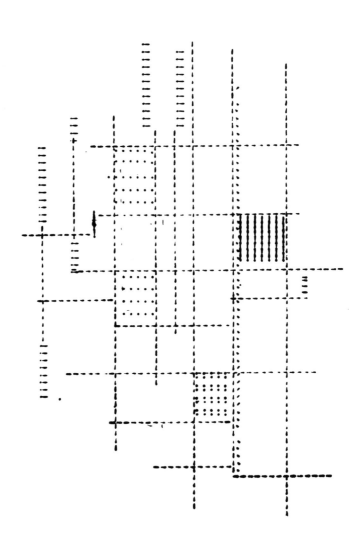

20   Typeprint H. N. Werkman (1923–29)

Typeprint   H. N. Werkman (1923–29)

22   Typeprint   H. N. Werkman (1923–29)

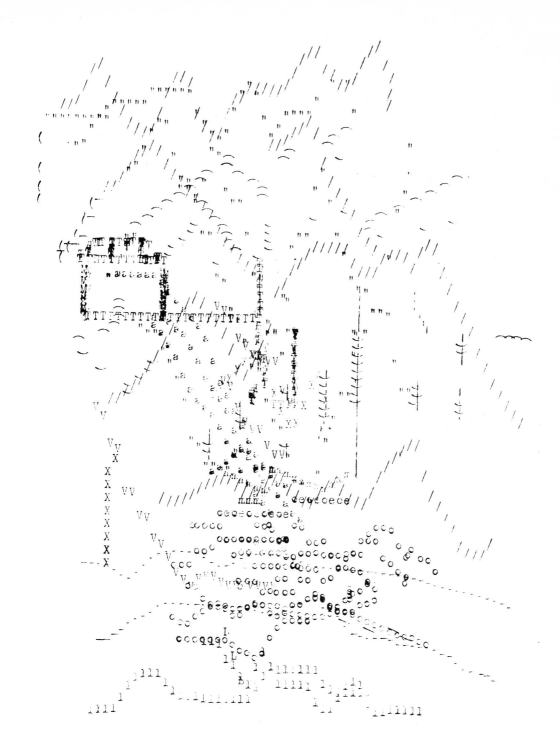

Typeprint   H. N. Werkman (1923–29)

24   Typeprint   H. N. Werkman (1923–29)

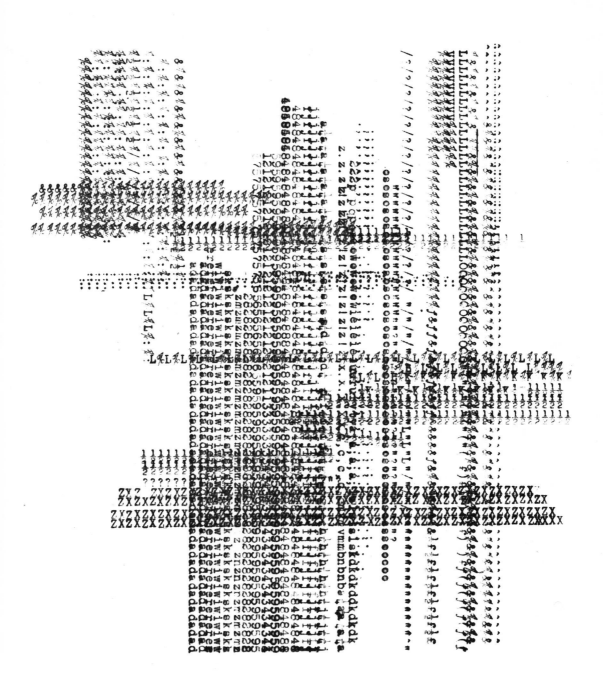

Typeprint   H. N. Werkman (1923–29)

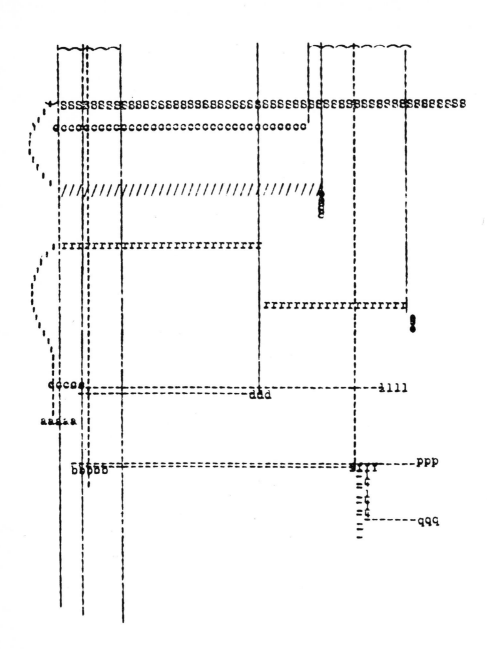

Typeprint   H. N. Werkman (1923–29)

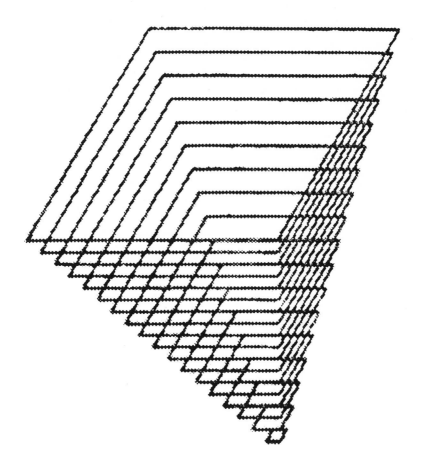

Construction exercise   Bauhaus student (mid-1920s)

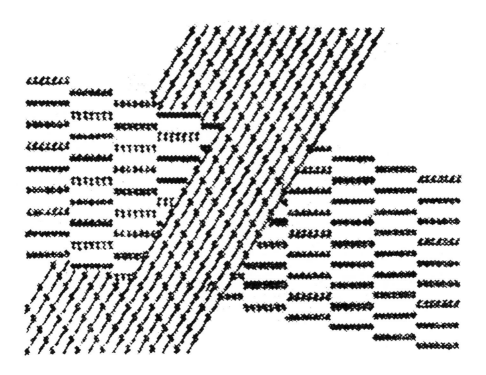

28   Construction exercise   Bauhaus student (mid-1920s)

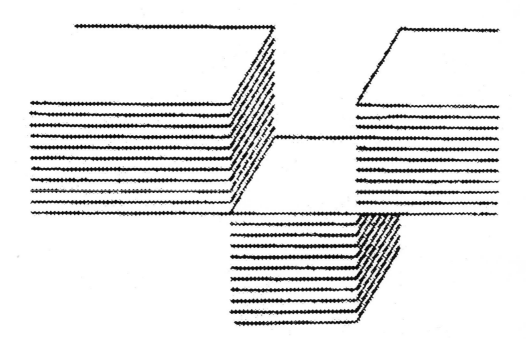

Construction exercise   Bauhaus student (mid-1920s)

30   Composition   Pietro de Saga (1926)

Contemporaries

Leaflikebird   Jeremy Adler (1969)

34   Light   Pierre Garnier and Seiichi Niikuni (1966)

Fountain (*Fontana*)   Jiří Kolář (1961)

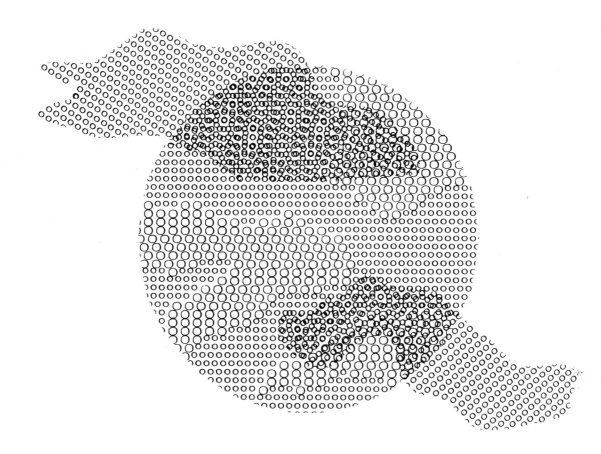

36   Texture poem for the moons of stars   Peter Finch (1971)

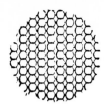

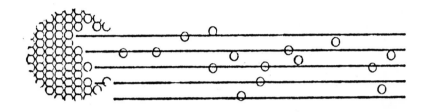

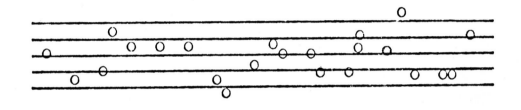

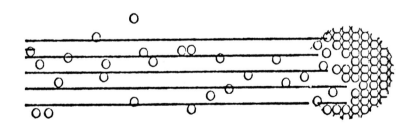

Moon song   Tristan Gray Hulse (1973)

Cityscape   Simon Parritt (1972)

Cityscape   Donato Cinicolo (1972)

40   Likecityscape   Jeremy Adler (1969)

Tinguely   Jiří Kolář (1962)

Brancusi   Jiří Kolář (1962)

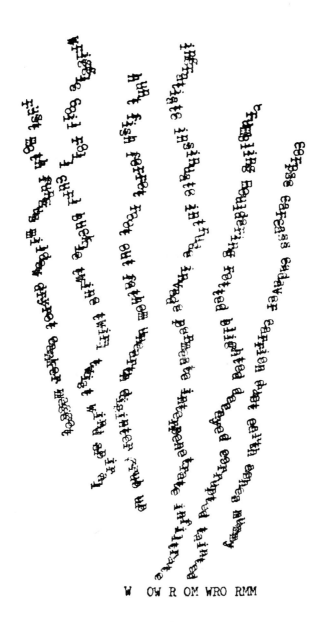

W   OW R OM WRO RMM

44   Worm   Bob Cobbing (1964)

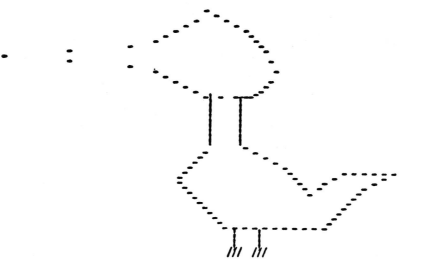

Bird   Henri Chopin (1955)

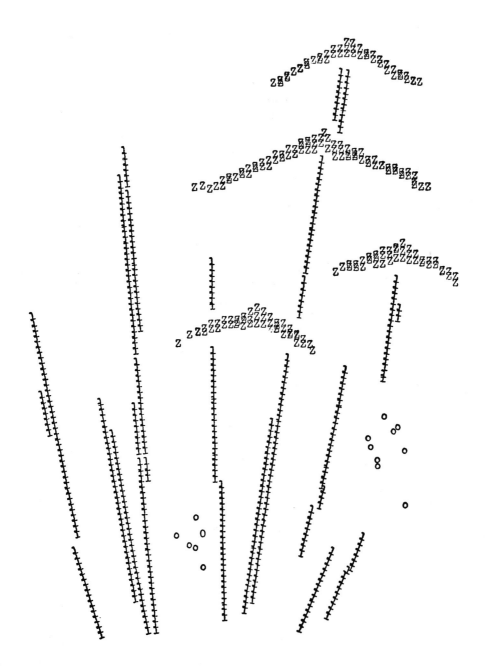

Defeat of the Teutonic Knights at Tannenberg   Ilse and Pierre Garnier (1966)

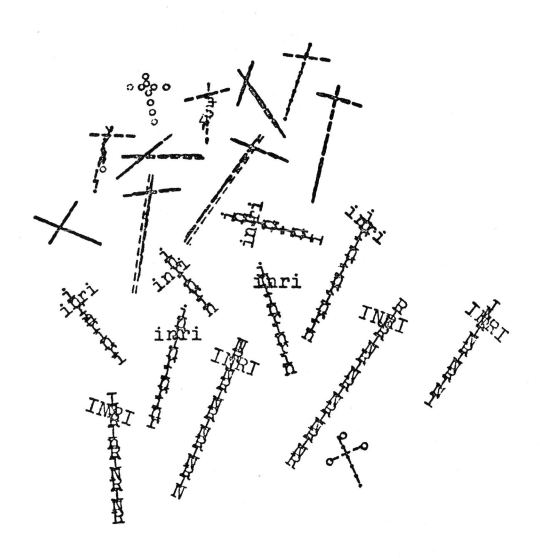

Arise the dead (*Debout les morts*)   Paul de Vree (1967)

Infantryman   Claus Bremer (1968)

```
                    All        es
     i kie    riskieren   s  ere
   s  Es  s Es     Es Es Es Es Es
   n  er ienen verdienen verdienen
   'a'am'am'am'am'am'am'am'am'am'a
   hluss Schluss Schluss Schluss Schlu
   alles alles alles alles alles alles
   zu zu zu zu zu zu zu zu zu zu zu z
   n erreichen erreichen erreichen er    hen  er
   lles Alles Alles Alles Alles Alle  Alles Al es A
   ufs aufs aufs aufs aufs aufs a  s aufs aufs au
   l Spiel Spiel Spiel Spiel Spi l Spiel Spiel S
   tzen setzen setzen setzen  setzen setzen setz
   'Alle'Alle'Alle'Alle'Alle'Alle'Alle'Alle'A
   rucken Brucken Brucken Brucken Brucken B   en
   r hinter hinter hinter hinter hinter h   er hin
   ch sich sich sich sich sich sich sic  ich sich
   n abbrechen abbrechen abbrechen abbr chen abbr
    'Sich'Sich'Sich'Sich'Sich'Sich'Sich'Sich'Si'
    durch durch durch durch durch durch durc
    e die die die die die die die die die die
    ole Parole Parole Parole Parole Pa
    rale
   rieg Krieg              eg Krieg Krieg Krieg Krieg Kr     Krie
   f au  auf auf          uf auf auf auf auf auf    auf a
   leb  eben le           en Leben Leben Leben Leben L  en Le
   nd u      nd und u     nd und und und und und und und und
   Tag u    Tag  Tag u   Tag Tag Tag Tag Tag Tag Tag Tag Tag
   eden jeden jeden jede       n jeden jeden jeden jeden jeden jeden
   n möglichen mög ichen möglichen möglichen möglichen mögli
   ückzug Ruckzug Ruckzug Ruckzug Ruckzug Ruckzug R
   en abschneiden abschneiden abschneiden abschneiden absc
   nen Einen Einen Einen Einen Einen Einen Einen Einen E
   eg Krieg Krieg Krieg Krieg Krieg Krieg Krieg Krieg K
   uhren fuhren fuhren fuhren fuhren fuhren fuhren fuhr
   det'det'det'det'det'det'det'det'det'det'det'det'de'
   einen keinen keinen keinen keinen keinen keinen k
   illstand Waffenstillstand Waffenstillstand Waffe
   'kein'kein'kein'kein'kein'kein'kein'kein'kein'
   hen Zuruckweichen Zuruckweichen Zuruckweich
   d und und und und und und und und und und
   en keinen keinen keinen keinen keinen k
   usgleich Ausgleich Ausgleich Ausgleich
   hr mehr mehr mehr mehr mehr mehr meh
   st zulasst zulasst zulasst zulass
   'Siegen'Siegen'Siegen'Siegen'S'
   eisst heisst heisst heisst
    'ipiell'prinzipiell'prin'
    zu zu zu zu zu zu z
    akzeptieren akze
     ss'd    das'
      da     s d
     en Leben
    icht nicht ni
    das d      das
    hoch      ste
    Gut
    ist
     ..
```

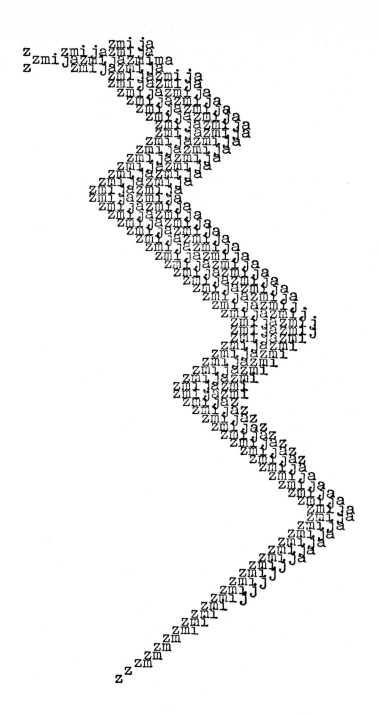

50   Snake (*Zmija*)   Miroljub Todorović (1971)

```
lllllllllllllllllllllllllluuuuuuuuuuuuuuuuuuuuuuuuuuuvvvvvvvvvvvvvvvvvvv
llllllllllllllllllllllllluuuuuuuuuuuuuuuuuuuuuuuuuuuvvvvvvvvvvvvvvvvvvvv
llllllllllllllllllllllluuuuuuuuuuuuuuuuuuuuuuuuuuuuvvvvvvvvvvvvvvvvvvvv
lllllllllllllllllllllluuuuuuuuuuuuuuuuuuuuuuuuuuuvvvvvvvvvvvvvvvvvvvvv
llllllllllllllllllluuuuuuuuuuuuuuuuuuuuuuuuuuuuvvvvvvvvvvvvvvvvvvvvvv
lllllllllllllllluuuuuuuuuuuuuuuuuuuuuuuuuuuuuvvvvvvvvvvvvvvvvvvvvvvv
lllllllllllllluuuuuuuuuuuuuuuuuuuuuuuuuuuuvvvvvvvvvvvvvvvvvvvvvvvvv
llllllllllluuuuuuuuuuuuuuuuuuuuuuuuuuuuvvvvvvvvvvvvvvvvvvvvvvvvvvv
llllllllluuuuuuuuuuuuuuuuuuuuuuuuuuuuuvvvvvvvvvvvvvvvvvvvvvvvvvvvv
llllllllluuuuuuuuuuuuuuuuuuuuuuuuuuuvvvvvvvvvvvvvvvvvvvvvvvvvvvvvvv
lllllllllluuuuuuuuuuuuuuuuuuuuuuuuuuvvvvvvvvvvvvvvvvvvvvvvvvvvvvvv
lllllllllllluuuuuuuuuuuuuuuuuuuuuuuuuuvvvvvvvvvvvvvvvvvvvvvvvvvvv
lllllllllllllluuuuuuuuuuuuuuuuuuuuuuuuuuvvvvvvvvvvvvvvvvvvvvvvvvv
llllllllllllllllluuuuuuuuuuuuuuuuuuuuuuuuuuvvvvvvvvvvvvvvvvvvvvvv
lllllllllllllllllllluuuuuuuuuuuuuuuuuuuuuuuuuuvvvvvvvvvvvvvvvvvvv
llllllllllllllllllllllluuuuuuuuuuuuuuuuuuuuuuuuuvvvvvvvvvvvvvvvvv
lllllllllllllllllllllllllluuuuuuuuuuuuuuuuuuuuuuuuuvvvvvvvvvvvvvvv
llllllllllllllllllllllllllllluuuuuuuuuuuuuuuuuuuuuuuuvvvvvvvvvvvvv
llllllllllllllllllllllllllllllllluuuuuuuuuuuuuuuuuuuuuuuuuuvvvvvvvvvvv
llllllllllllllllllllllllllllllllllluuuuuuuuuuuuuuuuuuuuuuuuuuvvvvvvvvv
lllllllllllllllllllllllllllllllllluuuuuuuuuuuuuuuuuuuuuuuuuuvvvvvvvvv
lllllllllllllllllllllllllllluuuuuuuuuuuuuuuuuuuuuuuuuuvvvvvvvvvvvvv
llllllllllllllllllluuuuuuuuuuuuuuuuuuuuuuuuuuuvvvvvvvvvvvvvvvvvvvv
llllllllllluuuuuuuuuuuuuuuuuuuuuuuuuuuuvvvvvvvvvvvvvvvvvvvvvvvvvv
llllllllluuuuuuuuuuuuuuuuuuuuuuuuuuuuuvvvvvvvvvvvvvvvvvvvvvvvvvvv
lllllllllluuuuuuuuuuuuuuuuuuuuuuuuuuuuvvvvvvvvvvvvvvvvvvvvvvvvvv
lllllllllllluuuuuuuuuuuuuuuuuuuuuuuuuuuvvvvvvvvvvvvvvvvvvvvvvvvv
lllllllllllllluuuuuuuuuuuuuuuuuuuuuuuuuuuvvvvvvvvvvvvvvvvvvvvvvv
llllllllllllllllluuuuuuuuuuuuuuuuuuuuuuuuuuuvvvvvvvvvvvvvvvvvvvv
llllllllllllllllllluuuuuuuuuuuuuuuuuuuuuuuuuuuvvvvvvvvvvvvvvvvvv
lllllllllllllllllllllluuuuuuuuuuuuuuuuuuuuuuuuuuuuvvvvvvvvvvvvvv
llllllllllllllllllllllllluuuuuuuuuuuuuuuuuuuuuuuuuuuuvvvvvvvvvvvv
llllllllllllllllllllllllllluuuuuuuuuuuuuuuuuuuuuuuuuuuuuvvvvvvvvvvv
llllllllllllllllllllllllllllluuuuuuuuuuuuuuuuuuuuuuuuuuuuuvvvvvvvvv
lllllllllllllllllllllllllllllllluuuuuuuuuuuuuuuuuuuuuuuuuuuvvvvvvvvv
lllllllllllllllllllllllllllllllllllluuuuuuuuuuuuuuuuuuuuuuuuuuvvvvvvvvv
lllllllllllllllllllllllllllllluuuuuuuuuuuuuuuuuuuuuuuuuuuuvvvvvvvvvv
lllllllllllllllllllllluuuuuuuuuuuuuuuuuuuuuuuuuuvvvvvvvvvvvvvvvvvvv
lllllllllllllllluuuuuuuuuuuuuuuuuuuuuuuvvvvvvvvvvvvvvvvvvvvvvvvvvv
llllluuuuuuuuuuuuuuuuuuuuuuuuuuuuuvvvvvvvvvvvvvvvvvvvvvvvvvvvvvvvv
llllllluuuuuuuuuuuuuuuuuuuuuuuuuuuuvvvvvvvvvvvvvvvvvvvvvvvvvvvvvvv
lllllllluuuuuuuuuuuuuuuuuuuuuuuuuuuuuvvvvvvvvvvvvvvvvvvvvvvvvvvvv
lllllllllluuuuuuuuuuuuuuuuuuuuuuuuuuuuvvvvvvvvvvvvvvvvvvvvvvvvvv
llllllllllllluuuuuuuuuuuuuuuuuuuuuuuuuuuvvvvvvvvvvvvvvvvvvvvvvvv
lllllllllllllluuuuuuuuuuuuuuuuuuuuuuuuuuuuuvvvvvvvvvvvvvvvvvvvvv
lllllllllllllllluuuuuuuuuuuuuuuuuuuuuuuuuuuuuvvvvvvvvvvvvvvvvvvv
llllllllllllllllllluuuuuuuuuuuuuuuuuuuuuuuuuuuuvvvvvvvvvvvvvvvvv
llllllllllllllluuuuuuuuuuuuuuuuuuuuuuuuuuuuuvvvvvvvvvvvvvvvvvvvv
llllllllluuuuuuuuuuuuuuuuuuuuuuuuuuuuvvvvvvvvvvvvvvvvvvvvvvvvvvvv
llllluuuuuuuuuuuuuuuuuuuuuuuuuuuuuuvvvvvvvvvvvvvvvvvvvvvvvvvvvvvvv
```

52   The honey pot   Alan Riddell (1969)

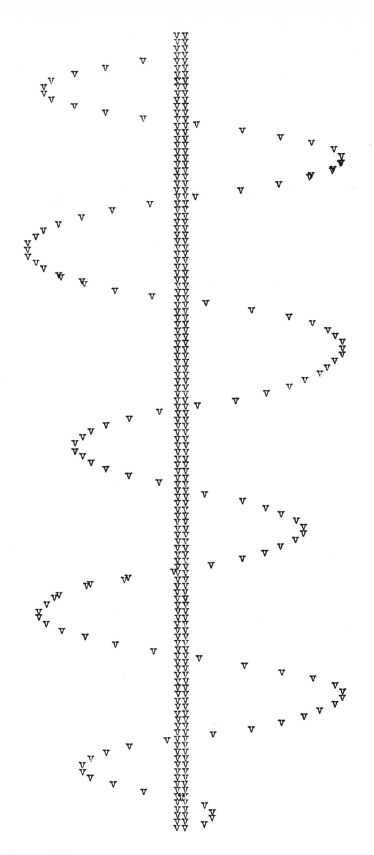

Vines   Ilse and Pierre Garnier (1972)

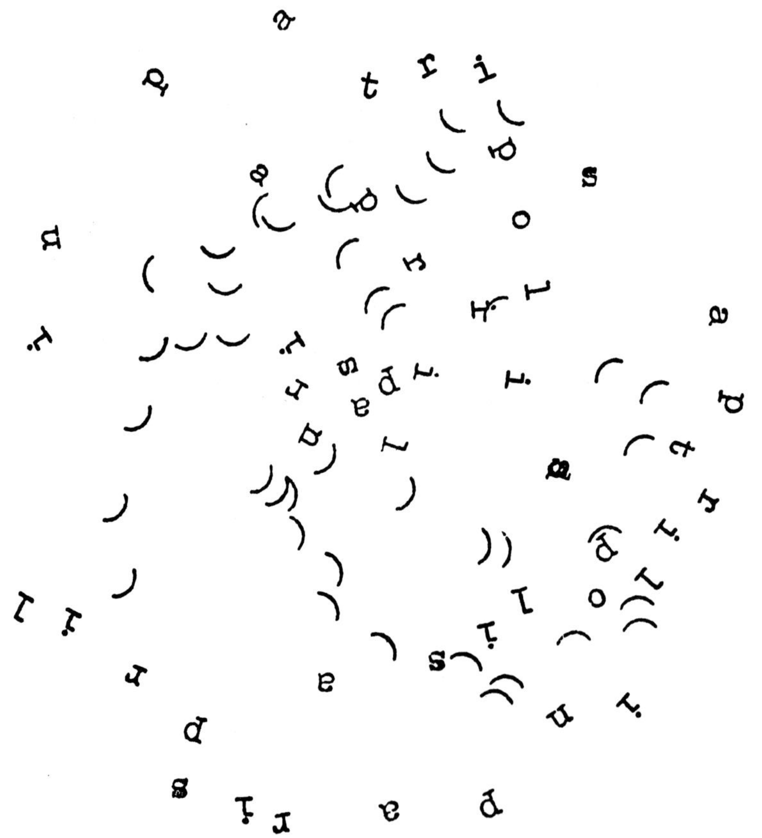

Untitled Paul de Vree (1966)

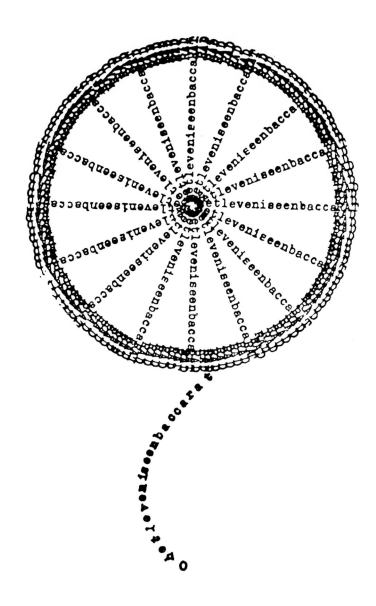

Life is a lottery (*Het leven is een baccarat*)   Paul de Vree (1966)

56   Section through a tree-trunk   J. P. Ward (1971)

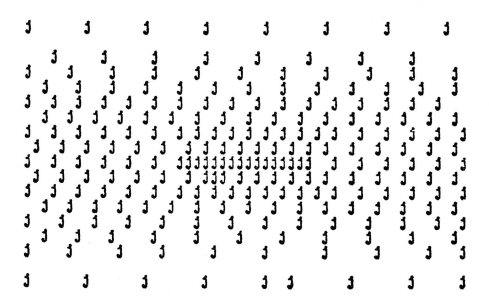

Vegetal sign   Ilse and Pierre Garnier (1965)

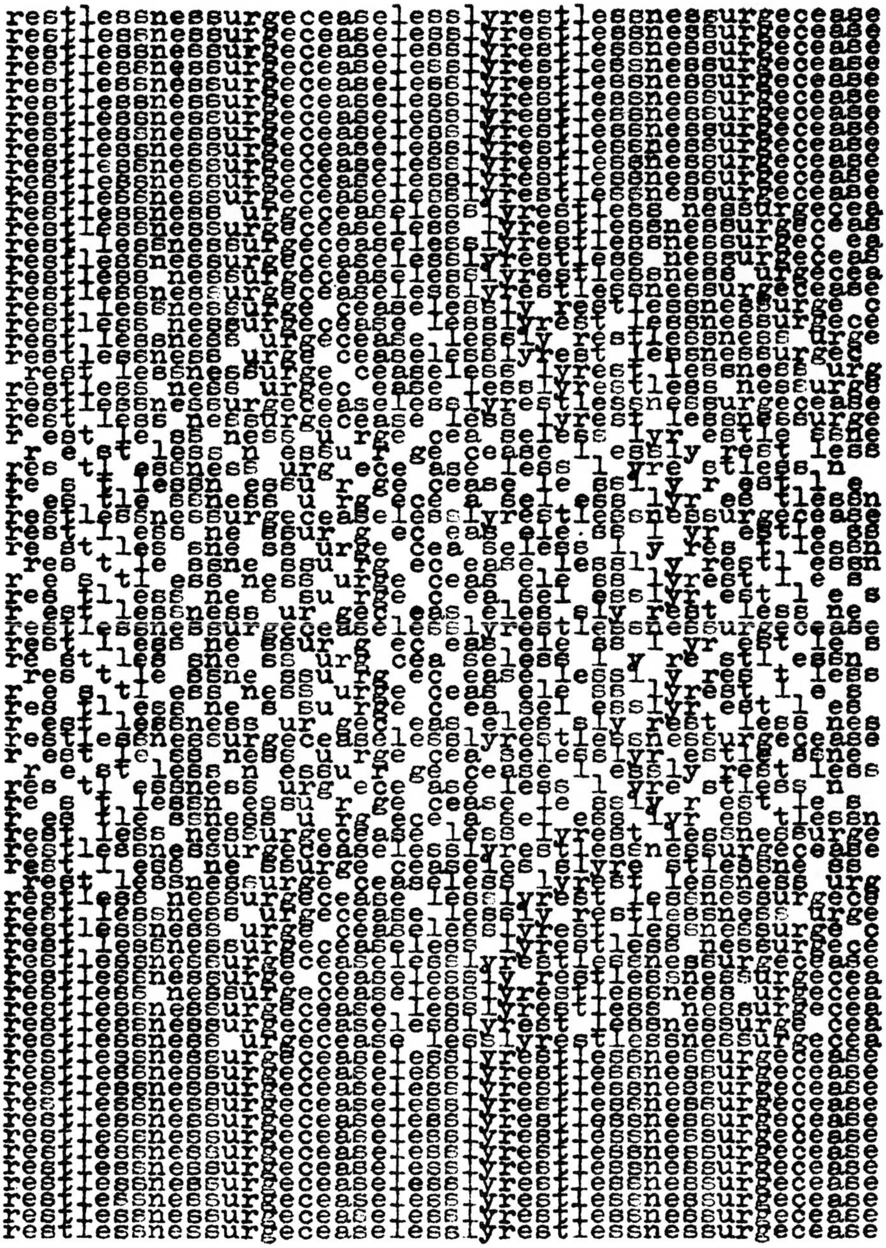
restlessnessurgeceaselesslyrestlessnessurgecease

60   Moon loom   Tristan Gray Hulse (1973)

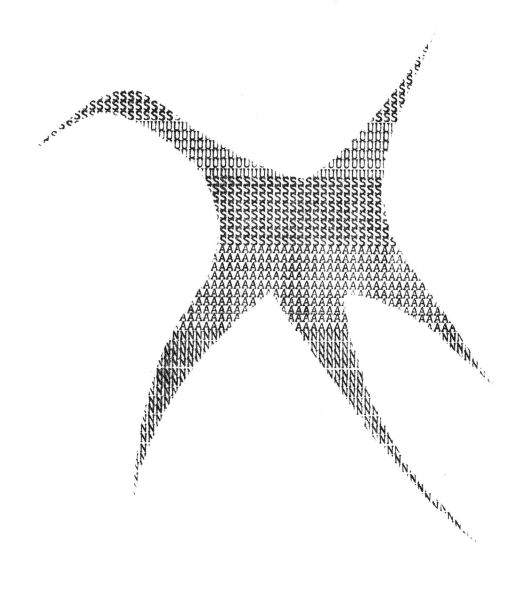

Susan   Robert Caldwell (1973)

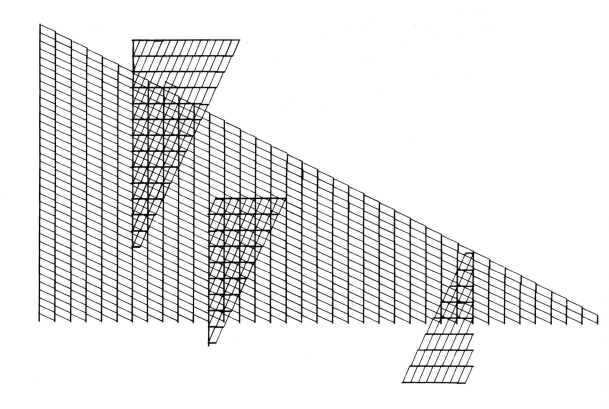

Grid 4   Simon Parritt (1971)

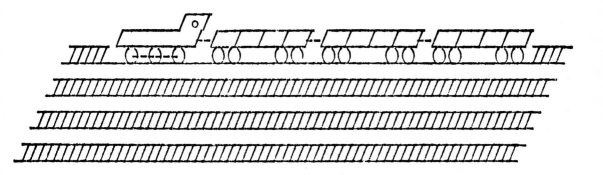

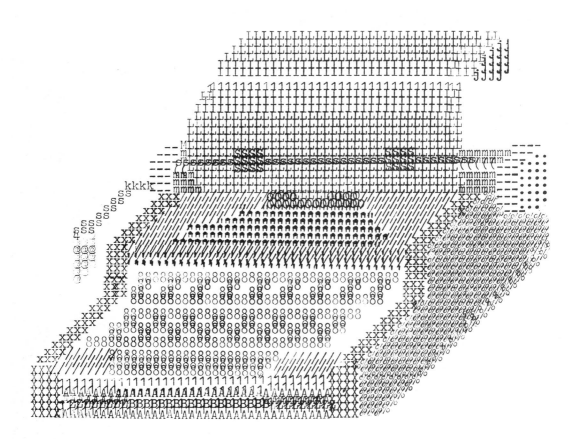

64   Typewriter   Gary Blake (1974)

Police dog Tosca   Will Hollis (1957)

66   Arab   Will Hollis (1946)

Portrait of the artist's wife   Zoran Popović (1969)

68   Gandhi   Iqbal Fareed (1969)

Copy, by Charlotte Hofton, of Dennis W. A. Collins' Churchill (1951) used as exercise by London College of Secretaries

The Duke of Edinburgh   Dennis W. A. Collins (1957)

Queen Elizabeth   Dennis W. A. Collins (1953)

72   Henri Chopin   Robert Morgan (1974)

```
wat wat wat wat wat wat wat wat wat w
ik ik ik ik ik ik ik ik ik ik ik ik i
mij mij mij mij mij mij mij mij mij m
herinner herinner herinner herinner h
zijn zijn zijn zijn zijn zijn zijn zi
schoten schoten schoten schoten schot
en en en en en en en en en en en en e
nog nog nog nog nog nog nog nog nog n
eens eens eens eens eens eens eens ee
schoten schoten schoten schoten schot
en en en en en en en en en en en en e
bommen bommen bommen bommen bommen bb
en en en en en en en en en en en en e
branden branden branden branden brand
en en en en en en en en en en en en e
lijken lijken lijker lijken lijken li
en en en en en en en en en en en en e
tranen tranen tranen tranen tranen tr
puin puin puin puin puin puin puin pu
en en en en en en en en en en en en e
een een een een een een een een een e
zee zee zee zee zee zee zee zee zee z
van van van van van van van van van v
bloed bloed bloed bloed bloed bloed b
en en en en en en en en en en en en e
graven graven graven graven graven gr
en en en en en en en en en en en en e
steeds steeds steeds steeds steeds st
meer meer meer meer meer meer meer me
schoten schoten schoten schoten schot
en en en en en en en en en en en en e
bommen bommen bommen bommen bommen bb
en en en en en en en en en en en en e
branden branden branden branden brand
en en en en en en en en en en en en e
lijken lijken lijken lijken lijken li
en en en en en en en en en en en en e
```

Announcement (*Anzeige*)   Klaus Peter Dencker (1971)

Space (*Spazio*)   Arrigo Lora-Totino (1966)

76   Illustration from teleprinter novel *Informed Sources*   Willard S. Bain (1967)

I could of course cut
down on the paper yes
the paper for writing
the damn thing if I'm
careful and I don't w
aste too much of it I
can play with the pap
er cut down by one or
two reams it's true I
haven't calculated th
e paper yet but event
ually I'll have to it's quite obvious but let's calculate with cigarettes
for the time being if
a carton of cigarette
s costs $3.80 as I de
cided earlier plus th
e tax of course 6 cen
ts tax for a total of
3.86 then if I divide
18.25 by 3.86 I'll ha
ve the number of cart
ons that must be sacr
ificed for the chewin
g gum is it worth the sacrifice or shall I skip the whole thing in any ca
se it comes out 4.728
cartons of cigarettes
it would indeed be si
mpler to do without c
hewing gum but the mo
re you chew the bette
r you are and the les
s you smoke you'll fe
el better in the long
run particularly sinc
e you can't smoke and chew at the same time supposedly therefore it's a d
eal we sacrifice 4.72
8 cartons of cigarett
es for chewing gum ho
wever it will have to
be rounded off to 5 b
ecause it's impossibl
e to sacrifice an une
ven number so here we
go 3.86 multiplied by
5 gives us the sum of
19.80 to spend on che
wing gum now if 365 packs cost 18.25 for 19.80 we can get 396 packs of gu
m which is more of co
urse than one pack pe
r day since we have o
nly 365 days to consi
der but we'll solve t
his problem later for
the time being let us
simply say that we no
w have 396 packs of g
um Spearmint of cours
e it lasts much longer

clic
clic
clic
clic
clic
clic
clic
clic
clic
clic
clic
clic
clic
clic
clic
clic
clic
clic
clic
clic
clic
clic
v clic   clic
clic   clic
clic   clic
clic   clic
clic   clic
clic   clic
clic   clic
clic   clic
clic   clic
clic   clic
clic   clic
clic   clic
clic   clic
clic   clic
clic   clic
clic   clic
clic   clic
cilc   clic
clic   clic
clic clic
clic clic
clic   clic
clic   clic
clicclic
clic
clic
clic
clic
clic il est fermé

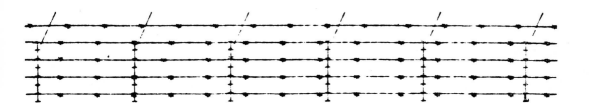

```
                              e
                            e e
                          e e e
      o o o o o o o o o ö ö ö ö o o o o o o o
      o o o o o o o o ö ö ö ö ö o o o o o o o
      o o o o o o o ö ö ö ö ö ö o o o o o o o
      o o o o o o ö ö ö ö ö ö ö o o o o o o o
      o o o o o ö ö ö ö ö ö ö ö o o o o o o o
      o o o o ö ö ö ö ö ö ö ö ö o o o o o o o
      o o o ö ö ö ö ö ö ö ö ö ö o o o o o o o
      o o ö ö ö ö ö ö ö ö ö ö ö o o o o o o o
      o ö ö ö ö ö ö ö ö ö ö ö ö o o o o o o o
      ö ö ö ö ö ö ö ö ö ö ö ö ö o o o o o o o
      e ö ö ö ö ö ö ö ö ö ö ö ö o o o o o o o
      e e ö ö ö ö ö ö ö ö ö ö ö o o o o o o o
      e e e e e e e e e e e e e e e e e
```

Condensation (*Zusammenfassung*)   Timm Ulrichs (early 1960s)

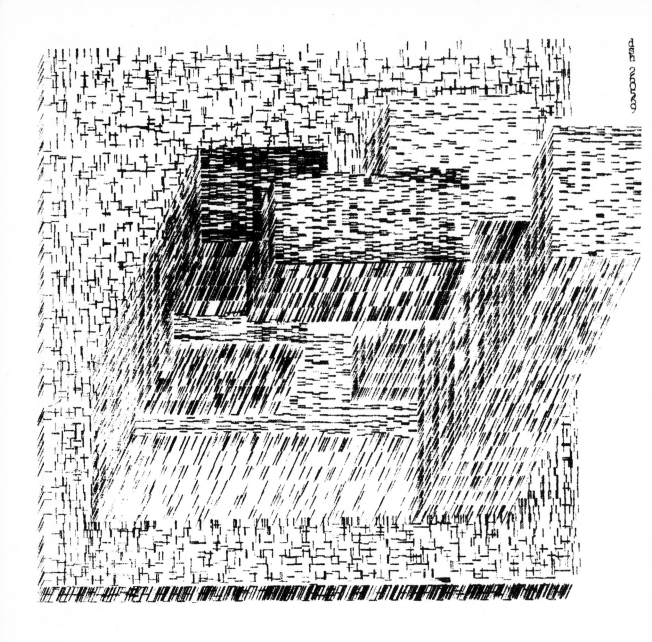

82   Typestract   Dom Sylvester Houédard (1969)

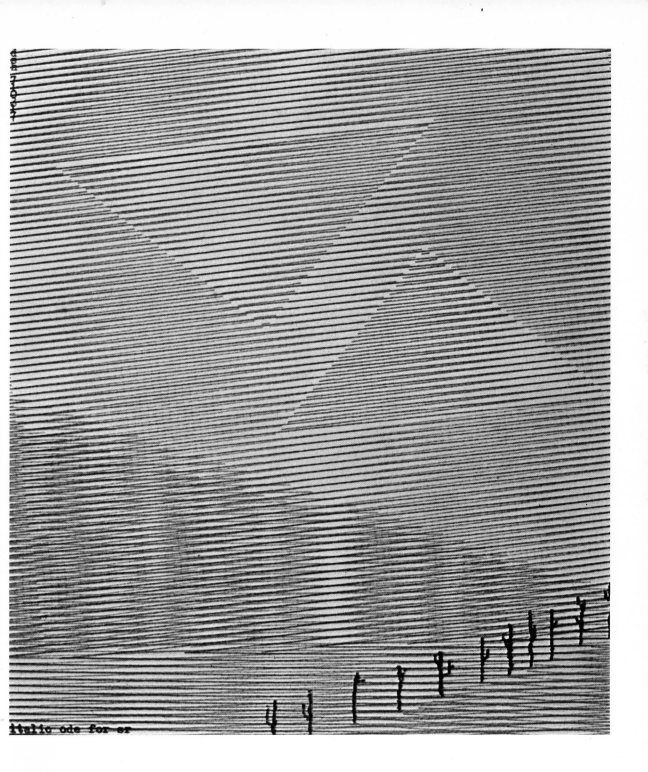

Italic ode   Dom Sylvester Houédard (1971)

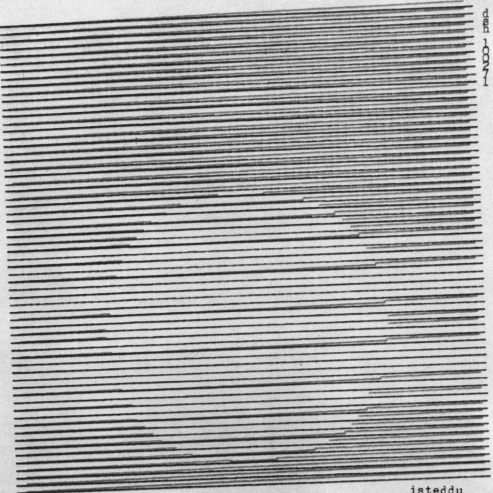

```
                                    isteddu
                              accurtu a se luna
                        tristu chi è deponne
```

```
    star / near the moon / sad is the one it strikes


    sardinian lovesong  //for the creative sadness of nino congiu
```

Typestract   Dom Sylvester Houédard (1972)

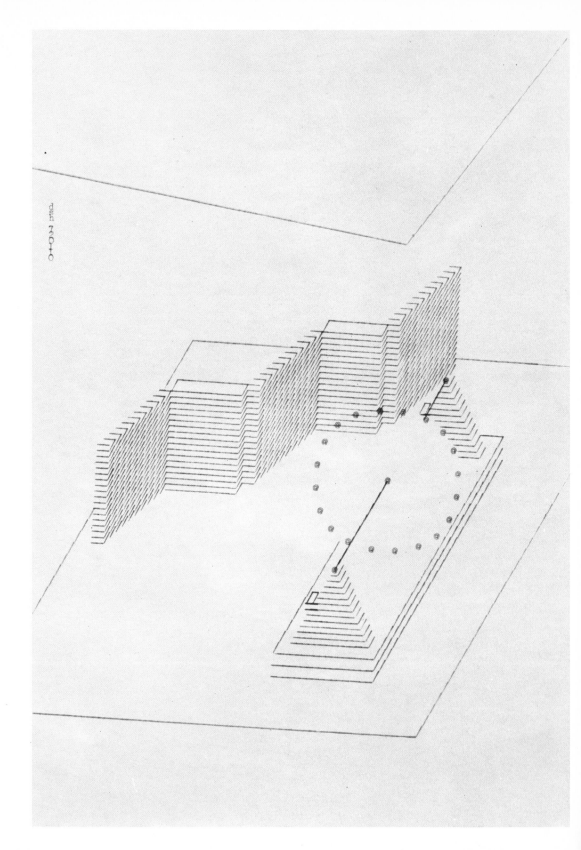

86   Typestract   Dom Sylvester Houédard (1972)

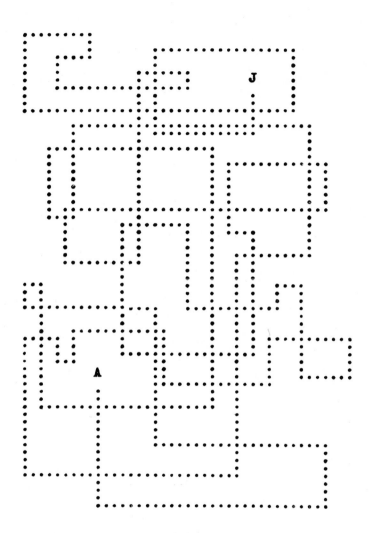

Estrangement   Václav Havel (mid-1960s)

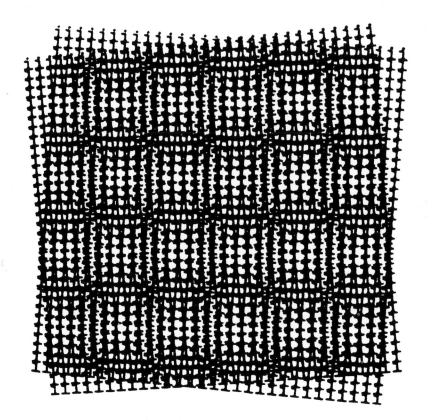

88   i   Jiří Valoch (1966)

A festive marching song in the shape of 10 dixie cups   Emmett Williams (1966)

```
g
 u
uuu
 u
      e
     ee
    eeeee
     ee
      e
         r
        rr
        rrr
       rrrrrrr
        rrr
         rr
          r
              1
              11
              111
              1111
            111111111
              1111
              111
              11
              1
                 1
                 11
                 111
                 1111
                 11111
              11111111111
                 11111
                 1111
                 111
                 11
                 1
                    1
                    11
                    111
                    1111
                    11111
                    111111
                 1111111111111
                    111111
                    11111
                    1111
                    111
                    11
                    1
                          a
                          aa
                          aaa
                          aaaa
                          aaaaa
                          aaaaaa
                          aaaaaaa
                    aaaaaaaaaaaaaaa
                          aaaaaaa
                          aaaaaa
                          aaaaa
                          aaaa
                          aaa
                          aa
                          a
```

Guerilla   Yüksel Pazarkaya (1971)

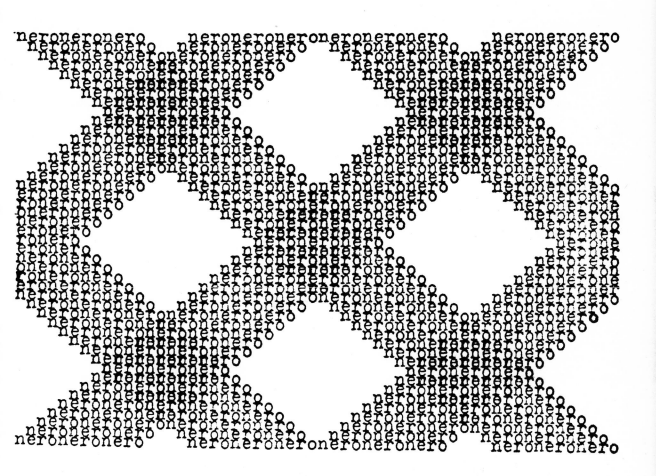

Black (*Nero*) Maurizio Nannucci (1964)

bianco bianc bian bia bi b bi bia bian bianc bianco
bianco bianc bian bia bi b bi bia bian bianc bianco
bianco bianc bian bia bi b bi bia bian bianc bianco
bianco bianc bian bia bi b bi bia bian bianc bianco
bianco bianc bian bia bi b bi bia bian bianc bianco
bianco bianc bian bia bi b bi bia bian bianc bianco
bianco bianc bian bia bi b bi bia bian bianc bianco
bianco bianc bian bia bi b bi bia bian bianc bianco
bianco bianc bian bia bi b bi bia bian bianc bianco
bianco bianc bian bia bi b bi bia bian bianc bianco
bianco bianc bian bia bi b bi bia bian bianc bianco
bianco bianc bian bia bi b bi bia bian bianc bianco
bianco bianc bian bia bi b bi bia bian bianc bianco
bianco bianc bian bia bi b bi bia bian bianc bianco
bianco bianc bian bia bi b bi bia bian bianc bianco
bianco bianc bian bia bi b bi bia bian bianc bianco
bianco bianc bian bia bi b bi bia bian bianc bianco
bianco bianc bian bia bi b bi bia bian bianc bianco
bianco bianc bian bia bi b bi bia bian bianc bianco
bianco bianc bian bia bi b bi bia bian bianc bianco
bianco bianc bian bia bi b bi bia bian bianc bianco
bianco bianc bian bia bi b bi bia bian bianc bianco
bianco bianc bian bia bi b bi bia bian bianc bianco
bianco bianc bian bia bi b bi bia bian bianc bianco
bianco bianc bian bia bi b bi bia bian bianc bianco
bianco bianc bian bia bi b bi bia bian bianc bianco
bianco bianc bian bia bi b bi bia bian bianc bianco
bianco bianc bian bia bi b bi bia bian bianc bianco
bianco bianc bian bia bi b bi bia bian bianc bianco
bianco bianc bian bia bi b bi bia bian bianc bianco
bianco bianc bian bia bi b bi bia bian bianc bianco
bianco bianc bian bia bi b bi bia bian bianc bianco
bianco bianc bian bia bi b bi bia bian bianc bianco
bianco bianc bian bia bi b bi bia bian bianc bianco
bianco bianc bian bia bi b bi bia bian bianc bianco
bianco bianc bian bia bi b bi bia bian bianc bianco
bianco bianc bian bia bi b bi bia bian bianc bianco
bianco bianc bian bia bi b bi bia bian bianc bianco
bianco bianc bian bia bi b bi bia bian bianc bianco
bianco bianc bian bia bi b bi bia bian bianc bianco
bianco bianc bian bia bi b bi bia bian bianc bianco
bianco bianc bian bia bi b bi bia bian bianc bianco
bianco bianc bian bia bi b bi bia bian bianc bianco
bianco bianc bian bia bi b bi bia bian bianc bianco
bianco bianc bian bia bi b bi bia bian bianc bianco
bianco bianc bian bia bi b bi bia bian bianc bianco
bianco bianc bian bia bi b bi bia bian bianc bianco
bianco bianc bian bia bi b bi bia bian bianc bianco
bianco bianc bian bia bi b bi bia bian bianc bianco
bianco bianc bian bia bi b bi bia bian bianc bianco
bianco bianc bian bia bi b bi bia bian bianc bianco
bianco bianc bian bia bi b bi bia bian bianc bianco
bianco bianc bian bia bi b bi bia bian bianc bianco
bianco bianc bian bia bi b bi bia bian bianc bianco
bianco bianc bian bia bi b bi bia bian bianc bianco
bianco bianc bian bia bi b bi bia bian bianc bianco
bianco bianc bian bia bi b bi bia bian bianc bianco
bianco bianc bian bia bi b bi bia bian bianc bianco
bianco bianc bian bia bi b bi bia bian bianc bianco
bianco bianc bian bia bi b bi bia bian bianc bianco
bianco bianc bian bia bi b bi bia bian bianc bianco
bianco bianc bian bia bi b bi bia bian bianc bianco
bianco bianc bian bia bi b bi bia bian bianc bianco
bianco bianc bian bia bi b bi bia bian bianc bianco
bianco bianc bian bia bi b bi bia bian bianc bianco
bianco bianc bian bia bi b bi bia bian bianc bianco
bianco bianc bian bia bi b bi bia bian bianc bianco
bianco bianc bian bia bi b bi bia bian bianc bianco
bianco bianc bian bia bi b bi bia bian bianc bianco
bianco bianc bian bia bi b bi bia bian bianc bianco
bianco bianc bian bia bi b bi bia bian bianc bianco

 White (*Bianco*) Maurizio Nannucci (1964)

giallo giallo giallo giallo giallo giallo giallo giallo giallo
giallo giallo giallo giallo giallo giallo giallo giallo giallo
giallo giallo giallo giallo giallo giallo giallo giallo giallo
giallo giallo giallo giallo giallo giallo giallo giallo giallo
giallo giallo giallo giallo giallo giallo giallo giallo giallo
giallo giallo giallo giallo giallo giallo giallo giallo giallo
giallo giallo giallo giallo giallo giallo giallo giallo giallo
giallo giallo giallo giallo giallo giallo giallo giallo giallo
giallo giallo giallo giallo giallo giallo giallo giallo giallo
giallo giallo giallo giallo giallo giallo giallo giallo giallo
giallo giallo giallo giallo giallo giallo giallo giallo giallo
giallo giallo giallo giallo giallo giallo giallo giallo giallo
giallo giallo giallo giallo giallo giallo giallo giallo giallo
giallo giallo giallo giallo giallo giallo giallo giallo giallo
giallo giallo giallo giallo giallo giallo giallo giallo giallo
giallo giallo giallo giallo giallo giallo giallo giallo giallo
giallo giallo giallo giallo giallo giallo giallo giallo giallo
giallo giallo giallo giallo giallo giallo giallo giallo giallo
giallo giallo giallo giallo giallo giallo giallo giallo giallo
giallo giallo giallo giallo giallo giallo giallo giallo giallo
giallo giallo giallo giallo giallo giallo giallo giallo giallo
giallo giallo giallo giallo giallo giallo giallo giallo giallo
giallo giallo giallo giallo giallo giallo giallo giallo giallo
giallo giallo giallo giallo giallo giallo giallo giallo giallo
giallo giallo giallo giallo giallo giallo giallo giallo giallo
giallo giallo giallo giallo giallo giallo giallo giallo giallo
giallo giallo giallo giallo giallo giallo giallo giallo giallo
giallo giallo giallo giallo giallo giallo giallo giallo giallo
giallo giallo giallo giallo giallo giallo giallo giallo giallo
giallo giallo giallo giallo giallo giallo giallo giallo giallo
giallo giallo giallo giallo giallo giallo giallo giallo giallo
giallo giallo giallo giallo giallo giallo giallo giallo giallo
giallo giallo giallo giallo giallo giallo giallo giallo giallo

Yellow (*Giallo*)   Maurizio Nannucci (1964)

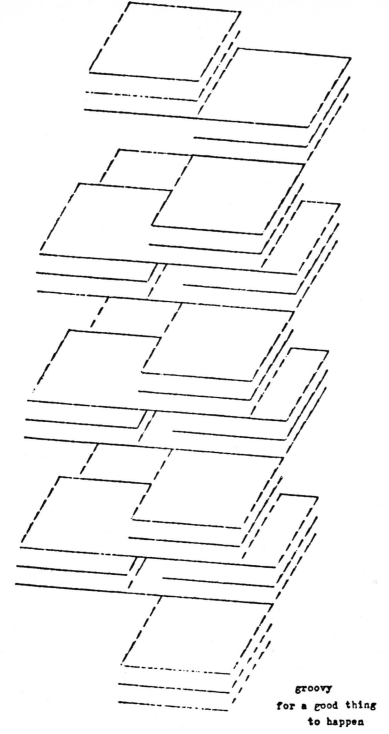

groovy
for a good thing
to happen

Typestract   Dom Sylvester Houédard (1971)

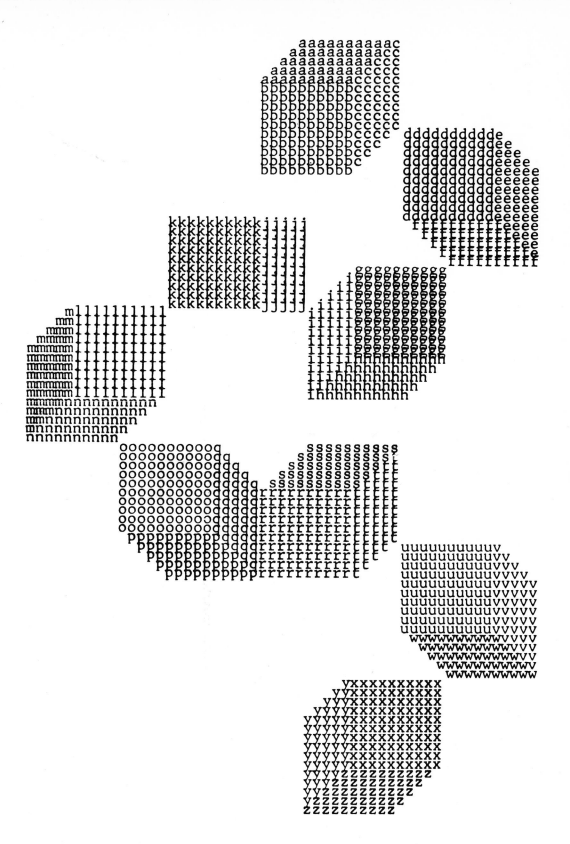

Homage to Vasarely   Alan Riddell (1971)

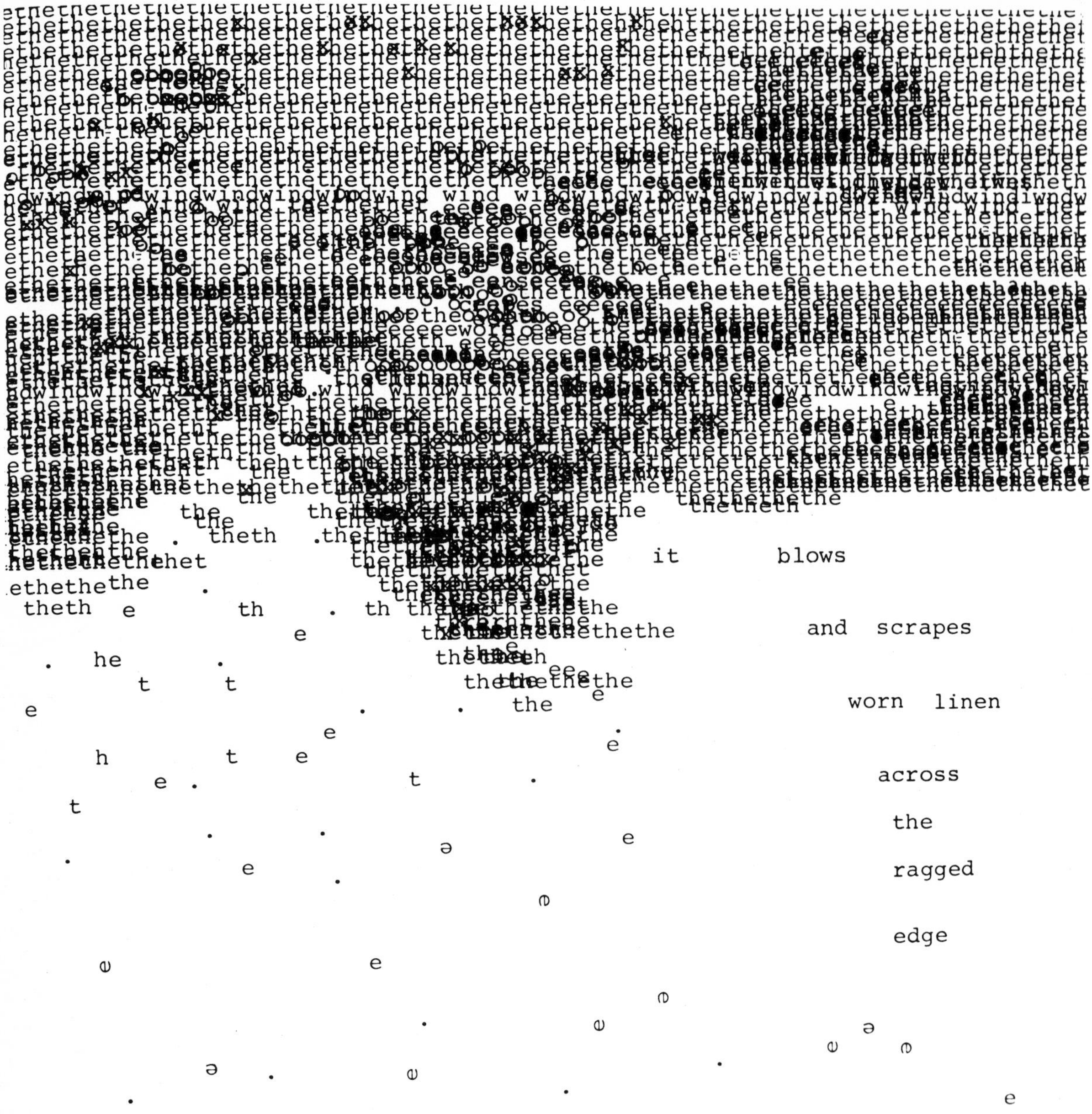
it blows
and scrapes
worn linen
across
the
ragged
edge

Untitled W. Bliem Kern (1973)

acco   ore   tobast   ,

                                                    k   ,

backcomebackcomebackcomebackcomebc

                                                                    c

        a

                            kcomebackcomebackcomebackcomebackcomebackcomebac

        when

you   jump

        through   time

            you

        lose

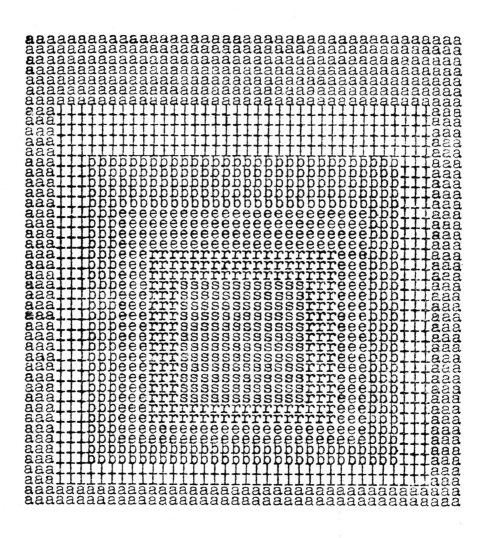

Albers   Jiřî Kolář (1962)

Facet of the 'Yin Yang' cube   Peter Mayer (1968)

Four other facets consist of the same design using the following pairs of symbols: ♀♂ ; 01 ; ? . ; | &. *The sixth facet has a verbal text*

oracular stupor

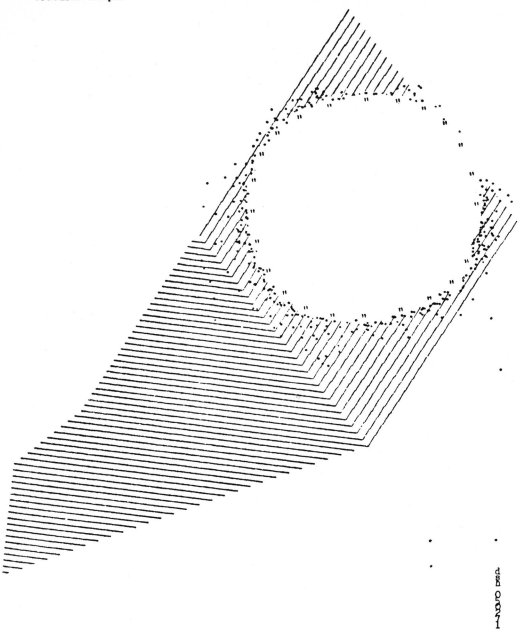

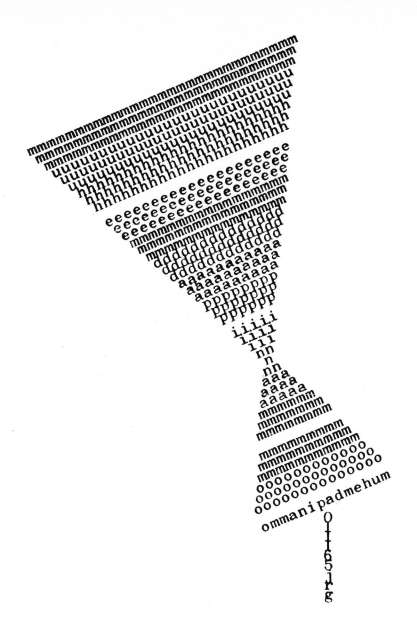

Buddhist mantra (*Om mani pad me hum*)   Robin Greer (1965)

目目目目目目瞑冥冥冥冥冥　　心心心心心目瞑冥相相相相
目目目目目目瞑冥冥冥冥冥　　心心心心目目瞑冥相相相相
目目目目目目瞑冥冥冥冥冥　　心心心目目目瞑冥冥相相相
目目目目目目瞑冥冥冥冥冥　　心心目目目目瞑冥冥冥相相
目目目目目目瞑冥冥冥冥冥　　心目目目目目瞑冥冥冥冥相
目目目目目目瞑冥冥冥冥冥　　目目目目目目瞑冥冥冥冥冥
心心心心心心想相相相相相　　相相相相相相想心心心心心
心心心心心心想相相相相相　　冥相相相相相想心心心心目
心心心心心心想相相相相相　　冥冥相相相相想心心心目目
心心心心心心想相相相相相　　冥冥冥相相相想心心目目目
心心心心心心想相相相相相　　冥冥冥冥相相想心目目目目
心心心心心心想相相相相相　　冥冥冥冥冥相想心目目目目

目目目目目目瞑冥冥冥冥冥　　目目目目目目瞑冥冥冥冥冥
相目目目目目瞑冥冥冥冥心　　心目目目目目瞑冥冥冥冥冥
相相目目目目瞑冥冥冥心心　　心心目目目目瞑冥冥冥相相
相相相目目目瞑冥冥心心心　　心心心目目目瞑冥冥相相相
相相相相目目瞑冥心心心心　　心心心心目目瞑冥冥相相相
相相相相相目瞑冥心心心心　　心心心心心目瞑冥相相相相
冥冥冥冥冥心想相目目目目　　冥冥冥冥冥相想心目目目目
冥冥冥冥心心想相相目目目　　冥冥冥冥相相想心心目目目
冥冥冥心心心想相相相目目　　冥冥冥相相相想心心心目目
冥冥心心心心想相相相相目　　冥冥相相相相想心心心心目
冥心心心心心想相相相相相　　冥相相相相相想心心心心心目
心心心心心心想相相相相相　　相相相相相相想心心心心心心

相相相相相目瞑冥心心心心　　目目目目目目瞑冥冥冥冥冥
相相相相目目瞑冥冥心心心　　目目目目目目瞑冥冥冥冥冥
相相相目目目瞑冥冥冥心心　　目目目目目目瞑冥冥冥冥冥
相相目目目目瞑冥冥冥冥心　　目目目目目目瞑冥冥冥冥冥
相目目目目目瞑冥冥冥冥心　　目目目目目目瞑冥冥冥冥冥
目目目目目目瞑冥冥冥冥冥　　目目目目目目瞑冥冥冥冥冥
心心心心心心想相相相相相　　相相相相相相想心心心心心
冥心心心心心想相相相相目　　相相相相相相想心心心心心
冥冥心心心心想相相相目目　　相相相相相相想心心心心心
冥冥冥心心心想相相目目目　　相相相相相相想心心心心心
冥冥冥冥心心想相目目目目　　相相相相相相想心心心心心
冥冥冥冥冥心想相目目目目　　相相相相相相想心心心心心

```
Polska kaszkę warzyła, temu dała,temu dała,temu dała, a temu żebek urwała, O!
 olska  aszkę  arzyła,  emu  ała, emu  ała, emu  ała,      emu ebek  rwała, O!
  lska   szkę   rzyła,   mu   ła,  mu   ła,  mu   ła,       mu  bek   wała, O!
   ska    zkę    zyła,    u    a,   u    a,   u    a,        u  ek    ała, O!
    ka     kę     yła,                                          k      ła, O!
     a      ę      ża,                                                 a, O!

     a      ę      ża,                                          k      ła, O!
    ka     kę     yła,    u    a,   u    a,   u    a,        u  ek    ała, O!
   ska    zkę    zyła,   mu   ła,  mu   ła,  mu   ła,       mu  bek   wała, O!
 olska  aszkę  arzyła,  emu  ała, emu  ała, emu  ała,      emu ebek  rwała, O!
Polska kaszkę warzyła, temu dała,temu dała,temu dała, a temu żebek urwała, O!
Polsk  kaszk  warzył , ten  dał ,ten  dał ,ten  dał , a ten  żebe  urwał , O!
Pols   kasz   warzy  , te   da  ,te   da  ,te   da  , a te   żeb   urwa  , O!
Pol    kas    warz   , t    d   ,t    d   ,t    d   , a t    że    urw   , O!
Po     ka     war.   ,              ,       ,   , a     ż     ur    , O!
P      k      wa     ,              ,       ,   , a           u     , O!

P      k      w      ,              ,       ,   , a                 O!
P      k      wa     ,              ,       ,   , a           u     , O!
Po     ka     war    ,              ,       ,   , e     ż     ur    , O!
Pol    kas    warz   , t    d   ,t    d   ,t    d   , a t    że    urw   , O!
Pols   kasz   warzy  , te   da  ,te   da  ,te   da  , a te   żeb   urwa  , O!
Polsk  kaszk  warzył , tem  dał ,tem  dał ,tem  dał , a ten  żebe  urwał , O!
Polska kaszkę warzyła, temu dała,temu dała,temu dała, a temu żebek urwała, O!
Polske kaszkę warzył , temu dała,temu dała,temu dała, a temu żebek urwała, O!
Polsk  kaszk  warzy  , temu dała,temu dała,temu dała, a temu żebek urwał , O!
Pols   kasz   warz   , temu dała,temu dała,temu dała, a temu żebe  urwa  , O!
Pol    kas    war    , tem  dał ,ten  dał ,ten  dał , a ten  żeb   urw   , O!
Po     ka     wa     , te   da  ,te   da  ,te   da  , a te   że    ur    , O!
P      k      w      , t    d   ,t    d   ,t    d   , a t    ż     u     , O!
Po     ka     wa     , te   da  ,te   da  ,te   da  , a te   że    ur    , O!
Pol    kas    war    , ten  dał ,ten  dał ,ten  dał , a ten  żeb   urw   , O!
Pols   kasz   warz   , temu dała,temu dała,temu dała, a temu żebe  urwa  , O!
Polsk  kaszk  warzy  , temu dała,temu dała,temu dała, a temu żebek urwał , O!
Polska kaszkę warzył , temu dała,temu dała,temu dała, a temu żebek urwała, O!
Polska kaszkę warzyła, temu dała,temu dała,temu dała, a temu żebek urwała, O!
Polska kaszkę  arzyła, temu dała,temu dała,temu dała,   temu żebek urwała, O!
 olska  aszkę  rzyła, temu dała,temu dała,temu dała,   temu żebek  rwała, O!
  lska   szkę   zyła, temu dała,temu dała,temu dała,   temu  ebek   wała, O!
   ska    zkę    yła, emu  ała, emu  ała, emu  ała, a emu   bek    ała, O!
    ka     kę     ża, mu   ła,  mu   ła,  mu   ła,       mu   ek     ła, O!
     a      ę      a,  u    a,   u    a,   u    a,        u   k      a, O!
```

St. Themerson, 1946.

Visual text   Stefan Themerson (1946)

Based on a traditional Polish nursery rhyme, the text reads : Poland cooked a pot of porridge. She gave some to this one, some to this one, and some to this one. And she wrang the neck of this one!

104   Towards me writing a book   Tom Edmonds (1970—71)

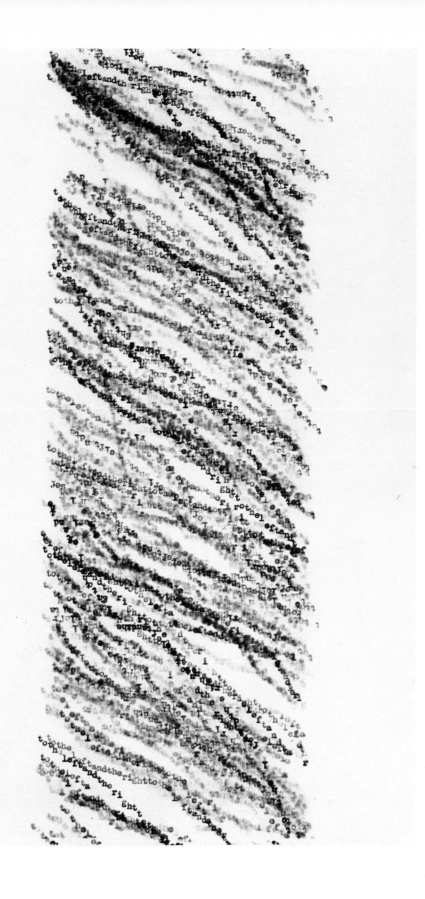

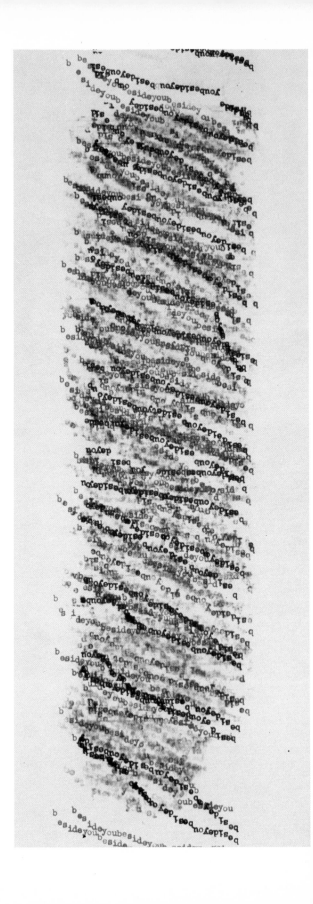

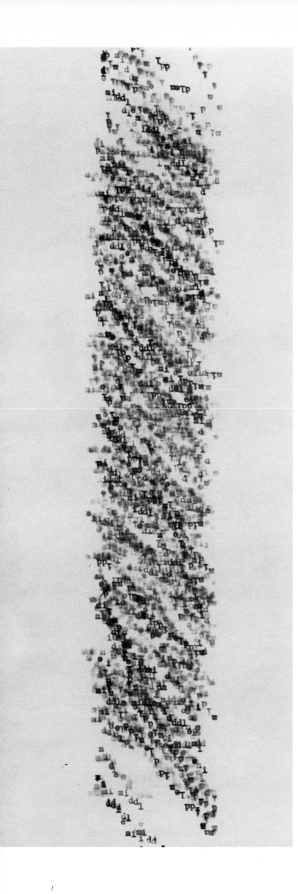
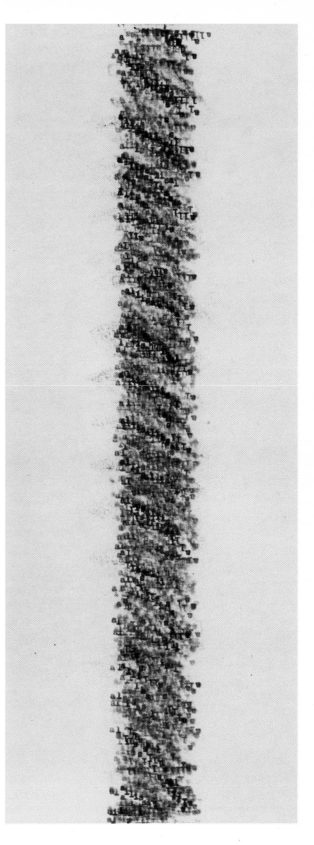

107

Two contiguous panels from 'Carnival'   Steve McCaffery (1967–70)

everywhere

ever

EVEVEVEVER
EVEVEVEVER
EYEYEYEYER
EYEYEYEYER
EYESEYEYES

NEXT
CAME EVE
WITH HER
CATEGORIES

WORM invertebrate limbless creeping animal some of which a
PARASITIC IN THE INTESTINES for example PARASITE LOUSED
also understood as an insignificant downtrodden person or s
DEBASED PERSON (the traw miltonic serpent,
assassin spiral part of screw also wurms waurms
wyrms
lies are directives

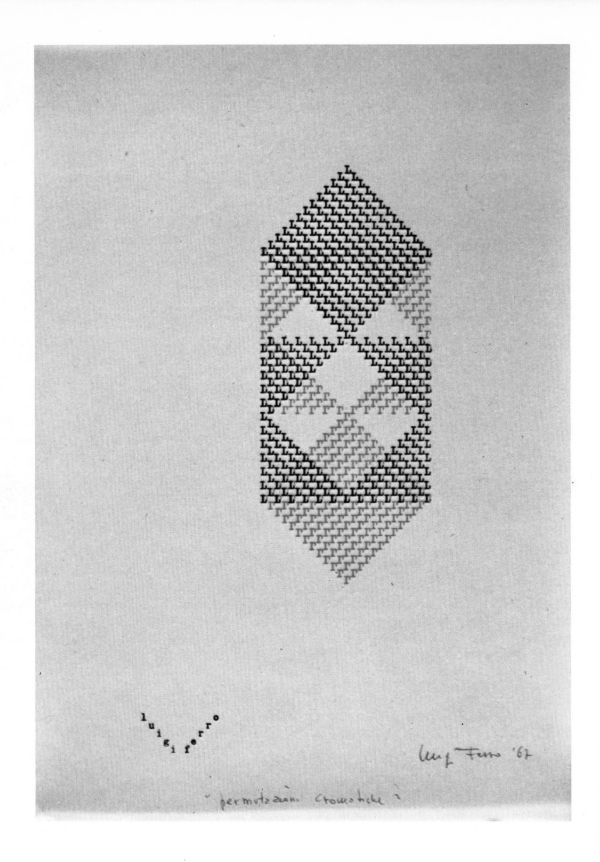

Chromatic permutations   Luigi Ferro (1967)

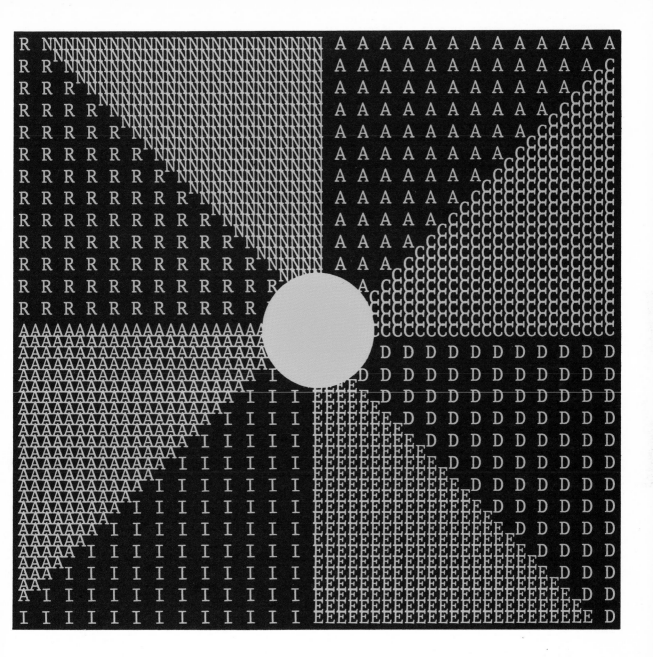

Aubade   Alan Riddell (1969)

WHITEWHITEWHITEWHITEWHITEWHITE
WHITEWHITEWHITEWHITEWHITEWHITE
WHITEWHITEWHITEWHITEWHITEWHITE
WHITEWHITEWHITE   WHITEWHITEWHITE
WHITEWHITEWHITE   WHITEWHITEWHITE
WHITEWHITEWHITE   WHITEWHITEWHITE
WHITEWHITE   WHITEWHITE
WHITEWHITE   WHITEWHITE
WHITEWHITE   WHITEWHITE
WHITEWHITEWHITE   WHITEWHITEWHITE
WHITEWHITEWHITE   WHITEWHITEWHITE
WHITEWHITEWHITE   WHITEWHITEWHITE
WHITEWHITEWHITEWHITEWHITEWHITE
WHITEWHITEWHITEWHITEWHITEWHITE
WHITEWHITEWHITEWHITEWHITEWHITE

ALASALAS   ALASALASALASALASALASALAS
ALASALAS   ALASALASALASALASALASALAS
ALASALAS   ALASALAS
ALASALAS   ALASALAS
                        ALASALASALASALASALAS
                        ALASALASALASALASALAS
ALASALAS   ALASALAS
ALASALAS   ALASALAS
ALASALAS   ALASALASALASALASALASALAS
ALASALAS   ALASALASALASALASALASALAS

ALASALASALASALASALASALASALASALASALAS
ALASALASALASALASALASALASALASALASALAS

ALASALASALASALASALASALASALASALASALAS
ALASALASALASALASALASALASALASALASALAS

Two flags   Alan Riddell (1968)

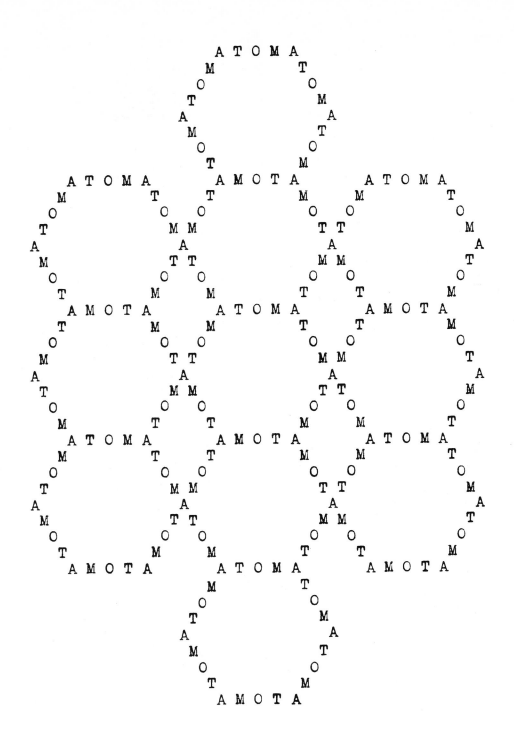

Anatomy of a tomato   Patrick Bridgwater (1967)

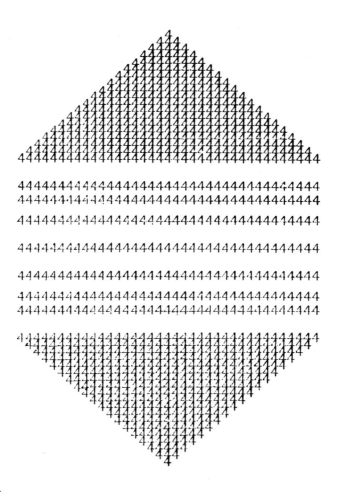

4444   Josef Hiršal (1968)

Untitled   Jiří Valoch (late 1960s)

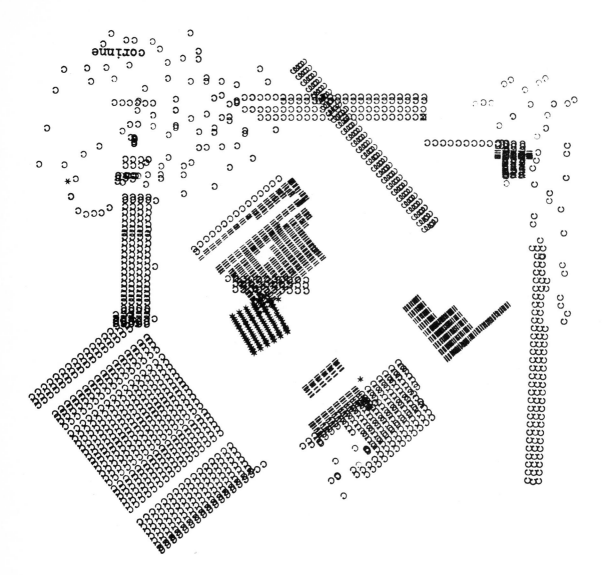

116   Untitled   Jiří Kolář (mid-1960s)

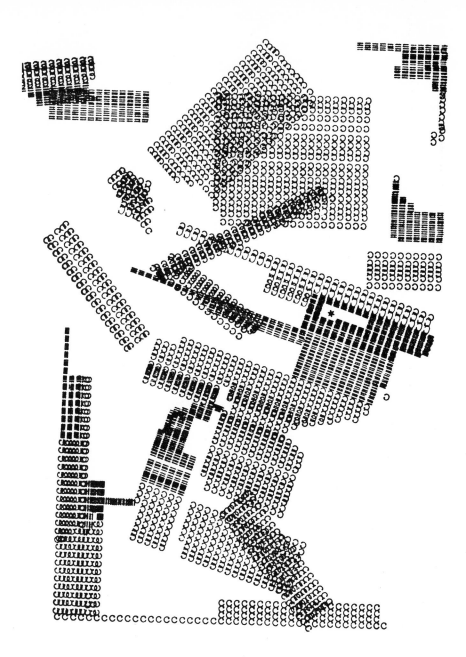

Untitled   Jiří Kolář (mid-1960s)

```
1 2 3 4 5 6 7 8 9 0 9 8 7 6 5 4 3 2 1
2 3 4 5 6 7 8 9 0 1 0 9 8 7 6 5 4 3 2
3 4 5 6 7 8 9 0 1 2 1 0 9 8 7 6 5 4 3
4 5 6 7 8 9 0 1 2 3 2 1 0 9 8 7 6 5 4
5 6 7 8 9 0 1 2 3 4 3 2 1 0 9 8 7 6 5
6 7 8 9 0 1 2 3 4 5 4 3 2 1 0 9 8 7 6
7 8 9 0 1 2 3 4 5 6 5 4 3 2 1 0 9 8 7
8 9 0 1 2 3 4 5 6 7 6 5 4 3 2 1 0 9 8
9 0 1 2 3 4 5 6 7 8 7 6 5 4 3 2 1 0 9
0 1 2 3 4 5 6 7 8 9 8 7 6 5 4 3 2 1 0
9 0 1 2 3 4 5 6 7 8 7 6 5 4 3 2 1 0 9
8 9 0 1 2 3 4 5 6 7 6 5 4 3 2 1 0 9 8
7 8 9 0 1 2 3 4 5 6 5 4 3 2 1 0 9 8 7
6 7 8 9 0 1 2 3 4 5 4 3 2 1 0 9 8 7 6
5 6 7 8 9 0 1 2 3 4 3 2 1 0 9 8 7 6 5
4 5 6 7 8 9 0 1 2 3 2 1 0 9 8 7 6 5 4
3 4 5 6 7 8 9 0 1 2 1 0 9 8 7 6 5 4 3
2 3 4 5 6 7 8 9 0 1 0 9 8 7 6 5 4 3 2
1 2 3 4 5 6 7 8 9 0 9 8 7 6 5 4 3 2 1
0 1 2 3 4 5 6 7 8 9 8 7 6 5 4 3 2 1 0
9 0 1 2 3 4 5 6 7 8 7 6 5 4 3 2 1 0 9
8 9 0 1 2 3 4 5 6 7 6 5 4 3 2 1 0 9 8
7 8 9 0 1 2 3 4 5 6 5 4 3 2 1 0 9 8 7
6 7 8 9 0 1 2 3 4 5 4 3 2 1 0 9 8 7 6
5 6 7 8 9 0 1 2 3 4 3 2 1 0 9 8 7 6 5
4 5 6 7 8 9 0 1 2 3 2 1 0 9 8 7 6 5 4
3 4 5 6 7 8 9 0 1 2 1 0 9 8 7 6 5 4 3
2 3 4 5 6 7 8 9 0 1 0 9 8 7 6 5 4 3 2
1 2 3 4 5 6 7 8 9 0 9 8 7 6 5 4 3 2 1
2 3 4 5 6 7 8 9 0 1 0 9 8 7 6 5 4 3 2
3 4 5 6 7 8 9 0 1 2 1 0 9 8 7 6 5 4 3
4 5 6 7 8 9 0 1 2 3 2 1 0 9 8 7 6 5 4
5 6 7 8 9 0 1 2 3 4 3 2 1 0 9 8 7 6 5
6 7 8 9 0 1 2 3 4 5 4 3 2 1 0 9 8 7 6
7 8 9 0 1 2 3 4 5 6 5 4 3 2 1 0 9 8 7
8 9 0 1 2 3 4 5 6 7 6 5 4 3 2 1 0 9 8
9 0 1 2 3 4 5 6 7 8 7 6 5 4 3 2 1 0 9
0 1 2 3 4 5 6 7 8 9 8 7 6 5 4 3 2 1 0
```

118   Mullions   Richard Kostelanetz (1970)

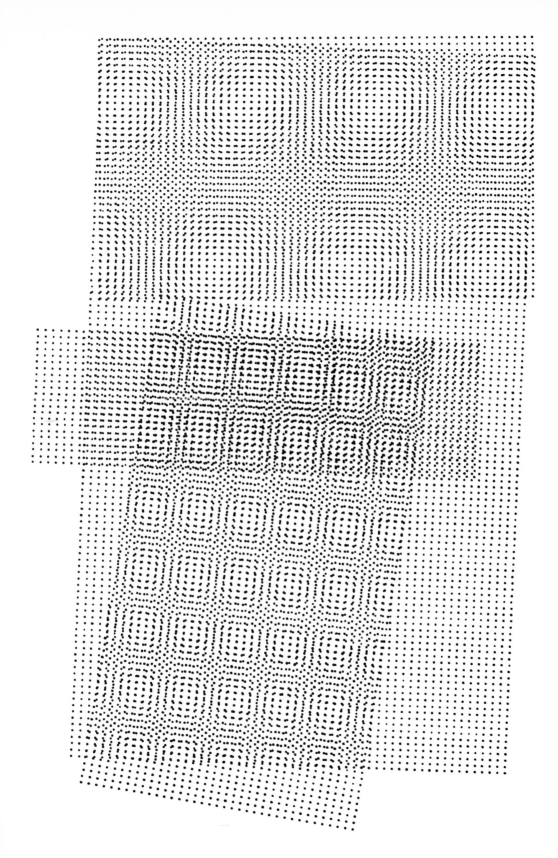

Typotexture   Timm Ulrichs (1962)

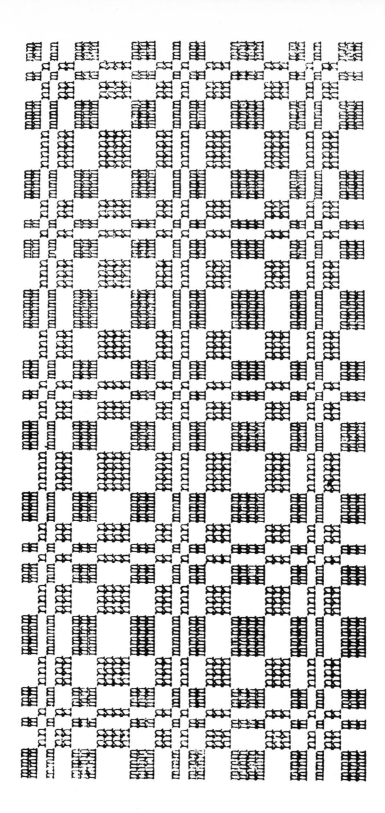

120   Poem for Rosemarie   Charles Cameron (1965)

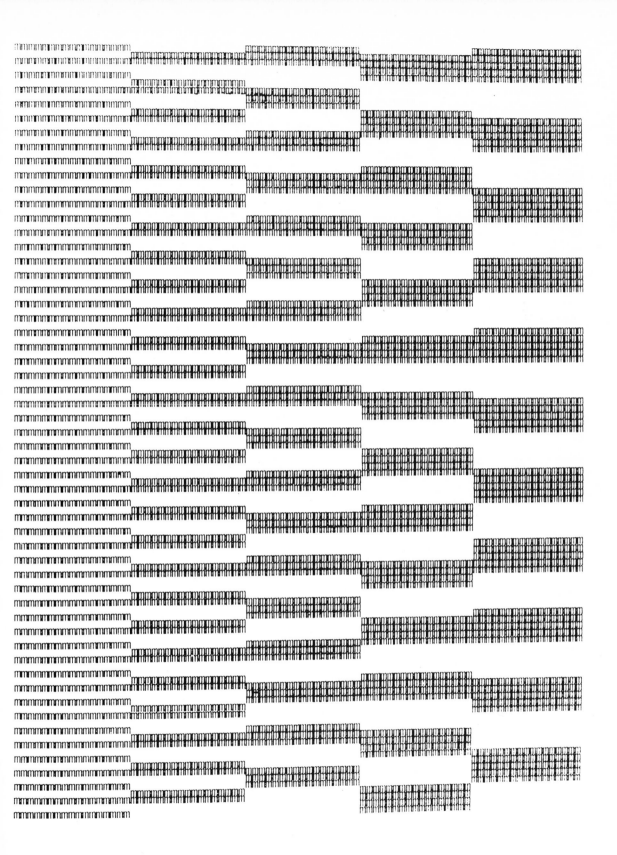

Untitled   Ilse and Pierre Garnier (1964)

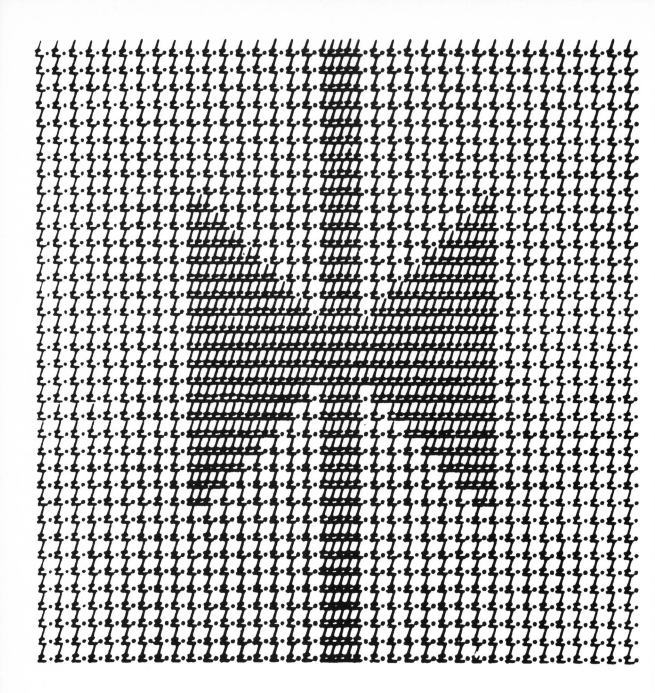

Untitled   Amelia Etlinger (1971)

Untitled   Amelia Etlinger (1971)

```
rrrrrrrrrrrrrrrrrrrrrrrrrrrrrrrrrrrrrrrrrrrrrrrrrrrrrrrrrrr
rrrrrrrrrrrrrrrrrrrrrrrrrrrrrrrrrrrrrrrrrrrrrrrrrrrrrrrrrr
rr                                                        rr
rreeeeeeeeeeeeeeeeeeeeeeeeeeeeeeeeeeeeeeeeeeeeeeeeeeeeee  rr
rreeeeeeeeeeeeeeeeeeeeeeeeeeeeeeeeeeeeeeeeeeeeeeeeeeeeee  rr
rree                                                ee  rr
rree tttttttttttttttttttttttttttttttttttttttttttttt  ee  rr
rree tt                                            tt ee  rr
rree tt                                            tt ee  rr
rree tt aaaaaaaaaaaaaaaaaaaaaaaaaaaaaaaaaaaaaaaaaa tt ee  rr
rree tt aaaaaaaaaaaaaaaaaaaaaaaaaaaaaaaaaaaaaaaaaa tt ee  rr
rree tt aa wwwwwwwwwwwwwwwwwwwwwwwwwwwwwwwww  aa tt ee  rr
rree tt aa wwwwwwwwwwwwwwwwwwwwwwwwwwwwwwwww  aa tt ee  rr
rree tt aa ww                            ww aa tt ee  rr
rree tt aa wwcccccccccccccccccccccccccc  ww aa tt ee  rr
rree tt aa wwcccccccccccccccccccccccccc  ww aa tt ee  rr
rree tt aa wwcc                      cc ww aa tt ee  rr
rree tt aa wwcc iiiiiiiiiiiiiiiiiiii  cc ww aa tt ee  rr
rree tt aa wwcc llllllllllllllllllll  cc ww aa tt ee  rr
rree tt aa wwcc ll              ll cc ww aa tt ee  rr
rree tt aa wwcc ll nnnnnnnnnnnnnnll cc ww aa tt ee  rr
rree tt aa wwcc ll nnnnnnnnnnnnnnll cc ww aa tt ee  rr
rree tt aa wwcc ll nn 000000000 nnll cc ww aa tt ee  rr
rree tt aa wwcc ll nn 000000000 nnll cc ww aa tt ee  rr
rree tt aa wwcc ll nn oo     oo nnll cc ww aa tt ee  rr
rree tt aa wwcc ll nn oossss oo nnll cc ww aa tt ee  rr
rree tt aa wwcc ll nn oossss oo nnll cc ww aa tt ee  rr
rree tt aa wwcc ll nn oossss oo nnll cc ww aa tt ee  rr
rree tt aa wwcc ll nn oo     oo nnll cc ww aa tt ee  rr
rree tt aa wwcc ll nn 000000000 nnll cc ww aa tt ee  rr
rree tt aa wwcc ll nn 000000000 nnll cc ww aa tt ee  rr
rree tt aa wwcc ll nnnnnnnnnnnnnnll cc ww aa tt ee  rr
rree tt aa wwcc ll nnnnnnnnnnnnnnll cc ww aa tt ee  rr
rree tt aa wwcc ll              ll cc ww aa tt ee  rr
rree tt aa wwcc lliiiiiiiiiiiiiiiiiill cc ww aa tt ee  rr
rree tt aa wwcc llllllllllllllllllll cc ww aa tt ee  rr
rree tt aa wwccccccccccccccccccccccccc  ww aa tt ee  rr
rree tt aa wwccccccccccccccccccccccccc  ww aa tt ee  rr
rree tt aa ww                            ww aa tt ee  rr
rree tt aa wwwwwwwwwwwwwwwwwwwwwwwwwwwwwww  aa tt ee  rr
rree tt aa wwwwwwwwwwwwwwwwwwwwwwwwwwwwwww  aa tt ee  rr
rree tt aa                                  aa tt ee  rr
rree tt aaaaaaaaaaaaaaaaaaaaaaaaaaaaaaaaaaaaaaaaaa tt ee  rr
rree tt aaaaaaaaaaaaaaaaaaaaaaaaaaaaaaaaaaaaaaaaaa tt ee  rr
rree tt                                            tt ee  rr
rree tttttttttttttttttttttttttttttttttttttttttttttt  ee  rr
rree                                                ee  rr
rreeeeeeeeeeeeeeeeeeeeeeeeeeeeeeeeeeeeeeeeeeeeeeeeeeeeee  rr
rreeeeeeeeeeeeeeeeeeeeeeeeeeeeeeeeeeeeeeeeeeeeeeeeeeeeee  rr
rr                                                        rr
rrrrrrrrrrrrrrrrrrrrrrrrrrrrrrrrrrrrrrrrrrrrrrrrrrrrrrrrrr
rrrrrrrrrrrrrrrrrrrrrrrrrrrrrrrrrrrrrrrrrrrrrrrrrrrrrrrrrrr
```

124   Sonic water   Dom Sylvester Houédard (1964)

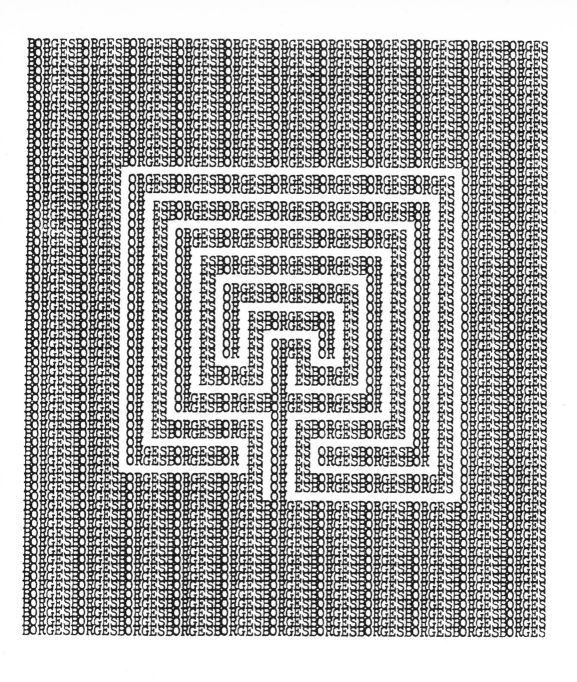

Labyrinth   Tim McDonough (1970)

126   Chromatic permutations   Luigi Ferro (1967)

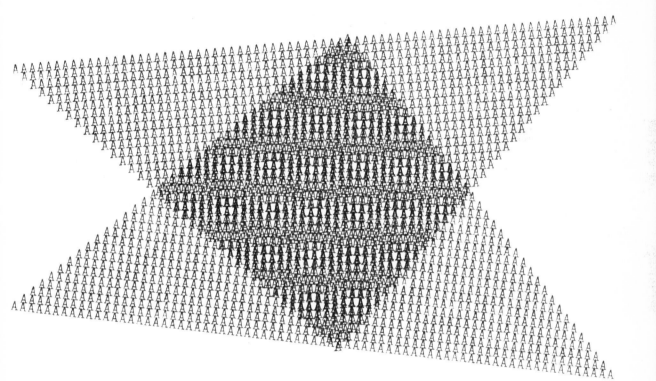

Chromatic permutations   Luigi Ferro (1967)

128   Chromatic permutations   Luigi Ferro (1967)

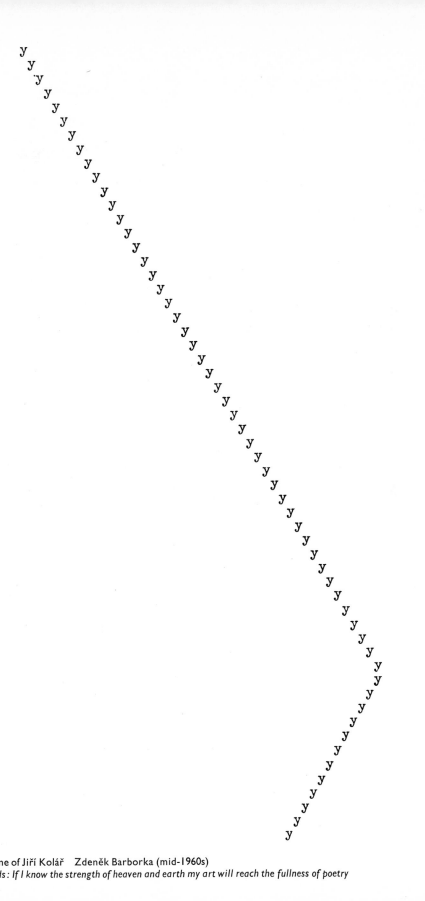

Nine meditations on a theme of Jiří Kolář   Zdeněk Barborka (mid-1960s)
The top line on page 137 reads: If I know the strength of heaven and earth my art will reach the fullness of poetry

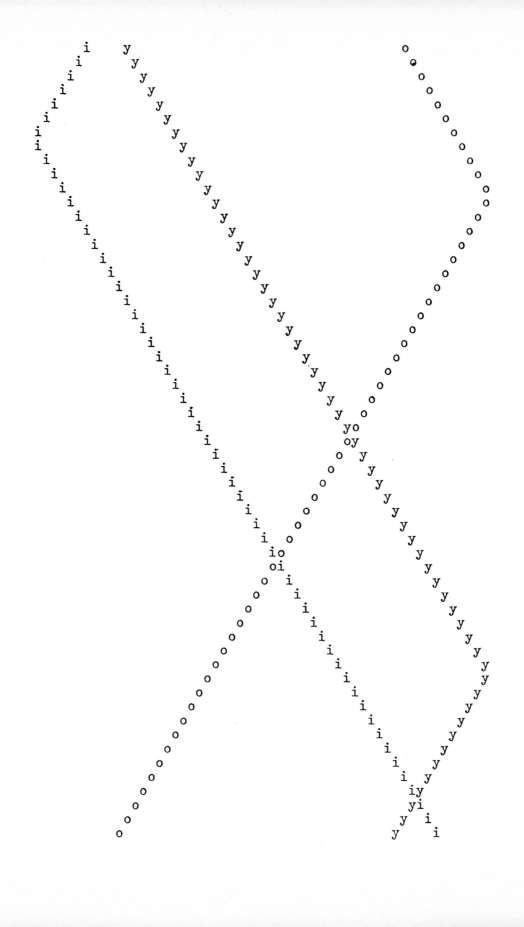

```
        is y       Z    é  m      h    lo.    e
        is  y      Z    é    m   mh  h     lo   e
         is   y   Z    é      m  h     lo  e
         is     yZ    é         mh       l oe
         is      yZ    é            mh        leo
         is       Zy   é            hm       el o
         is      Z  yé       h     m      e lo
        is      Z   yé       h      m      e  lo
        si     Z    éy       h       m      e   lo
        si    Z     é y      h        m      e    lo
         si   Z     é  y     h         m      e    lo
          si Z      é   y    h          me     lo
          s iZ      é    y   h          em      ol
          s iZ      é    yh             e m       o l
           sZi      é     hy            e  m       ol
           Zs ié          h   y         e   m      ol
          Z  s ié         h    y        e    m     ol
          Z   séi         h     y       e     m     ol
          Z    és i       h      y      e      mo l
         Z      é s i     h       y     e        oml
         Z      é  s i    h        ye             o lm
         Z      é   s ih            ey            o l m
         Z      é    s ih            e y          o l m
          Zé        shi              e   y        ol   m
          éZ        hs i             e    y        ol   m
         é  Z        h s i          e      y      o l    m
         é   Z       h  s i         e       y      ol      m
         é    Z      h   s i e            yo l       m
         é     Z h       s ie            oyl         m
          é     Zh        s ie           o ly        m
          é     hZ         sei           o l y         m
           é   h Z         es i          o l  y         m
            éh     Z       e s i        ol      y       m
            hé      Z      e  s i       ol       y      m
            h é      Z e      s i        ol        y  m
            h  é      Z e       si ol              ym
            h   é      Ze        s io l             my
            h    é      eZ        soil              m y
            h     é     e Z        osli            m    y
            h      ée    Z         o ls i         m      y
            h       eé    Z        ol si        m        y
             h       e é    Z   ol  si        m          y
              h       e  é    Z ol    si       m          y
               h      e   é    Zo l     s i m            y
                h     e    é    oZl      s im            y
                he         é  olZ         smi            y
                eh         é ol Z          ms i         y
                e h        oél    Z         m si        y
                 e h       o lé     Z        m si       y
                  e h     ol é       Z      m  si       y
                   e h    ol é        Z m      si      y
                    e     h ol        é     Zm      si y  y
                    e      ho l       é      mZ       si y
                     e       ohl      é  m  Z        s iy
                      e       o lh       ém   Z       syi
                       e       ol h      mé    Z      ys i
                        e      ol  h      mé    Z     y s i
```

132

```
       -is y e      Z  ě  é  m   d  he  lo        e
        -is   ye      Z  ěé    m  d  he   lo    e
        -is   ey    Z    éě     md  he     loe
        -is   e y z Z    é   ě   dm he      loe
       -is   e    yZ    é   ě  d mhe       leo
       -is   e    Zy    é    ěd  hme       el o
       i-s   e   Z y  é    dě h em       e l o
       is-   e   Z   yé    d  ěhem       e  lo
       si- e   Z    éy    d  hěe   m     e    lo
       si-e   Z    éy  d he ě    m  e       lo
       s ie-    Z   é  yd he  ě   m e        lo
        sei - Z   Ž é     yd  he      ě   me        lo
       es i -Z   é     dy he      ě  em        ol
       e  siZ-   é     d yhe        ě  em       ol
       e   sZi - é     d hye       ěe    m     ol
       e   Zs i -é     d  hey      eě    m    ol
       eZ  s ié-     d hey       eě    m   ol
        eZ   séi -   d he  y      e  ě    m ol
       Ze   és i -  d he   y     e   ě    mo l
       Z e  é s i-d he      y e       ě    mol
       Z  eé   s id- he      ye       ě   oml
       Z   ée   sdi -h e      ey        ě o lm
        Z  é e   ds ih-e      e y        oěl   m
        Zé    e d shie-       e  y        o lě    m
        éZ    ed hsei -        e    y      ol ě     m
        é  Z   de hes i-'       e     y    ol   ě     m
        é   Z d eh e s i-     e      y ol       ě    m
        é     Zd hee   s ï - e        yo l         ě   m
        é   dZ h ee    si -e        oyl          ě  m
        é  d Zh e e    sie-'        o ly          ěm
         éd   hZe   e    sei -        ol y          mě
        dé  h eZ    e    es i-'      ol   y         m ě
        d  éhe  Z   e  es i -      ol   y         m  ě
        d  hée   Z   ee  si -   ol       y       m   ě
        d h eé   Z   ee   si -ol        ym       ě
        d he  é    Z e  e    s io-1        my        ě
         dh e   é    Ze   e    soil-         m y      ě
         hde     é    eZ    e    osli-'        m   yě
         h ed      é e Z    e   ols i-'       m     ěy
         he  d     ée  Z    e  ols i-      m     ěy
         eh  d     eé    Z   eol si-      m     ě  y
         e h  de é     Z  oel  si-     m     ě   y
          e h  de   é    Z ole   si- m         ě    y
          e h  de      é    Zol e   si -m      ě     y
           e h  ed       é   oZl  e   sim-  ě        y
           e he  d       é o lZ    e    smi - ě        y
            eeh   d       éol  Z     e   ms i -ě        y
            ee h   d      oél   Z     e  ms iě-         y
           e eh   d    o lé    Z   em  sěi -          y
            e  eh  d o lé     Z  me  ěs i -         y
          e      eh  do l  é     Z me ě si -        y
          e        eh  odl     é    Zm  eě   si -   y
          e         e ho ld        é    mZ  ěe   si -y
          e          eohl  d        é m Z ě e    siy-
          e          oelh  d        ém  Zě    e    syi -
           e         o le h  d      mé  ěZ   e   ys i -
            e       ol eh d m é ě Z    e y si-
```

```
n - i s ly Ne      Z mě é m  d  heplo.      e   e
n- i s l  yeN      Zm éé    m d  hep lo'    e  e
 -ni s l  ey N   Z m  éě     md  he p      lo e  e
 - ins l   e  y NZ m  é  ě    dm  he p       loe  e
 - i snl   e    yZNm  é   ěd  mhe p         leo  e
 -i sln  e     ZymN  é    ěd  hme p         el oe
 i-s l  ne    Z my Né     dě h emp         e  leo
 is-l  en    Z m yéN    d  ěh e pm         e  el o
 sil-  e n   Z m  éy N    d  hěe p m       e   el o
 sli -e   nZ m  é y N d  h eěp  m       e  e   lo
 ls ie-   Znm  é   y Nd  h e pě      m  e  e    lo
 l sei - Z mn  é    ydN  h ep  ě      me   e     lo
  les i -Z m  né       dy Nh e p   ě       em  e      ol
  el s iZ-m  én       d  yhNe p        ě   e me      ol
  e  l sZim- é n      d  hyeNp         ěe   em      ol
  e  lZsmi -é  n   d  h eypN          eě  e m      ol
   e Zlms ié-     nd  h e py N         e  ěe   m    o l
   eZ ml séi -    dn  h e p y N        e  eě    m o l
   Zem lés i - d  nh e p   yN e  e  ě    mo l
   Z me él s i -d  hne p      y Ne   e    ě   oml
  Zm  eé  l s id- h enp          yeN  e       ě  o lm
  Zm  ée  l sdi -he pn         ey Ne        ěo l  m
 mZ  é e   lds ih-e p n      e  yeN         oěl    m
 m Zé   e  dl shie-p  n      e  ey N         o lě     m
  méZ     ed  lhseip-    n    e  ey N     ol  ě     m
  ém Z    de  hlespi-    ne  e   y N  ol   ě      m
 é m Z d  eh elps i -    en  e      y No l         ě    m
 é  m Zd  hee pl s i -  e  ne          yoNl         ě    m
 é   mdZ  h eep  ls i -e  en          oylN           ě m
  é  dm Zh e pe   l s ie- e  n       o ly N           ěm
   éd  mhZe e e   l sei -e   n      ol y N          mě
   dé  hmeZp   e  les ie-      n o l   yN          m ě
   d  éh empZ   e  el sei -     no l    yN  m     ě
   d  hée pm Z    ee  les i -    onl      yN m      ě
   d  h eép m Z    ee  el s i -  oln       y Nm      ě
   d  he pé   mZ  e ee  l s i -ol n       y mN     ě
   dh ep  é   m Ze  ee   l s io-l  n       my N ě
   hde p  é   meZ  e e   l soil-      n     m  y Ně
   h edp   é   em Ze   e   losli -     n   m    yěN
   he pd    ée  meZ   e  ollss i -     n m      ěy N
   ehp  d     eé  em Z    eo ll s i -    nm      ě y N
   eph  d   e   ée m Z    oel l s i -   mn      ě  y N
   pe h  d e   eé  mZ ole   l s i - m ně          y N
   p e h  de  e é   m Zo l e   l s i -m    ně          yN
    p eh ed e   é  moZl   e   l s im-      ěn            Ny
    p e h e  de     é  omlZ   e   l smi - ě n          N y
    p eeh  ed      éo l m Z   e   l ms i -ě  n         N y
     pee he  d     oél  m Z    e  ml s ię-     n N y
     ep eeh  d   o lé   mZ    em  l sěi -        nN y
     e  pee h  d o l é    m Z    me  lěs i -      Nny
      e  epeh  do l   é    mZ m e  ěl s i - N yn
      e  e peh  odl     é   m Zm   eě  l s i -Ny  n
      e  e   pe ho ld     é   mmZ    ěe   l s iN-y      n
      e  e     p eohl  d      é  mm Z ě  e . l sNiy-       n
      ee        poelh  d      ém  m Zě   e  lNsyi - n
      ee        ople h  d      mé  měZ     e  Nlys i -      n
      e  e      o lp e.h   d    m é  ěm Z     eN yl s i -  n
```

```
n m- i síly Ne    a Z mě  é  mn  do h e pl p.t pe  e
 n-mi s lí yeN  a Z m  ěé    mnd  oh e p  l o tp e   e
 -nims l íey Na Z m   éě     mdn hoe p    l opte   e
 - insml  eí yaNZ m    é  ě    dm nh eop      lpoet e
- i snlm e íayZNm    é   ě  d  mhne po       pleo te
-i s ln me  aíZymN    é    ěd  hmenp o    p el oet
i-s l nem a Zímy Né        dě  h empn  o  pe  leo t
is-l  en ma Z mí yéN      d  ěh e pm n   ope  el o t
sil- e namZ m íéy N      d  hěe p m n  poe  e l o t
sli -e  anZmm  éí y N  d  h eěp   m np eo  e    l o t
ls ie- a Znmm  é í y Nd  h e pě     mpne oe      lto
l sei -a Z mn mé   í ydN h e p  ě    pmen eo      tlo
les ia-Z m  ném    ídy Nh e p    ě  p em ne  o   t ol
el saiZ-m  én m   dí yhNe p      ěp e  men  o t o l
e lasZim- é n m  d íhyeNp      pěe   em n   ot o l
e alZsmi -é  n m d híeypN      p eě  e m n  too l
ea Zlms ié-    ndm h eípy N    p e  ěe   m nt ool
aeZ ml séi -    dn mh e pí y N  p e  eě    mtno lo
a Zem lés i -  d nhme p í y Npe  e  ě    tmonl o
aZ me él s i-d  hnemp    í ypNe  e   ě  t omln  o
Zam eé l s id- h enpm     ípyeN e    ět o lm n   o
Zma  ée  l sdi -h e pn m    píey Ne    těo l m n  o
mZ aé e  lds ih-e p n m  p eí yeN     t oěl   m no
m Zéa  e  dl shie-p  n mp e íey N   t o lě     mon
méZ a  ed lhseip-   npme  eí y N t o l ě    om n
ém Z a  de hlespi -   pnem e í y Nt o l    ě o  mn
é m Z ad  eh elps i - p en me   í ytNo l      ěo   nm
é  m Zda  hee pl s i -pe nem    ítyoNl     oě n m
é  mdZ ah eep  l s ip-e  en m  tíoylN     o ěn m
é  dm Zhae pe  l spie- e n m  t oíly N    o  něm
éd  mhZeap e  lpsei -e  n mt o lí y N  o   n mě
dé  hmeZpa  e  ples ie-    ntmo l  í y No   n m ě
d  éh empZ a  ep el sei -    tnoml  í yoN n m     ě
d  hée pm Z a  pee les i -  t onlm   íoy Nn m     ě
d  h eép  m Z ap ee  el s i -to ln m    oí ynNm     ě
d  h e pé  m Zpae ee  l s it-o l  n m o  ínymN    ě
dh e p é  mpZea  ee  l stio-l   n mo   nímy N ě
hde p   é  pmeZ ae  e  ltsoil-     nom  n mí y Ně
h edp    ép em Zea  e  tlosli -     on mn m  í yěN
he pd     pée  meZ a  et olls i - o  nnmm    íěy N
ehp d    p eé  em Z a  teo ll s i -o  nnmm    éí y N
eph   d  pe  ée  m Z at oel  ls io-  nmn m  ě íy N
pe h   dp e  eé  m Ztao le  l soi -n m  n mě   í y N
p e h  pde   e  é  mtZoal  e  los in-m   něm     í yN
p e hp ed  e  é  tmoZla  e  ol snim-    ěn m      íNy
 p ephe de    ét omlZ a  eo lnsmi -  ě n m      Níy
 ppeeh ed    téo lm Z a  oe nlms i -ě   n m   N yí
 ppee he  d  t oél  m Z ao en ml s iě-    n mN y í
 p ep eeh   d t o lé   m Zoa nem l sěi -     nNmy í
 pe  pee h  dt o l é  moZ an me  lěs i -    Nnymí
 pe  epeh  tdo l  é  om Znam e  ěl s i -  N yním
pe  e  pe ht odl    éo mnZma  eě  l s i -N y ín m
ep e    p etho ld    oé  nmmZ a  ěe  ls iN-y í  n m
e pe      pteohl d   o  én mm Z aě  e  l sNiy-í   nm
 eep     tpoelh  d  o  ném m Zěa  e  lNsyií-   mn
ee p    t ople h  do  n mé  měZ a  e  Nlysíi - m n
e e p  t o lpe h od nm é  ěm Z a   eN ylís i -m n
```

Zn m-li síly Ne e a Z mě é um ní do áh e pl oʼt poe ie
Z n-mils lí yeNe a Z m ěěu mínd oháe p l o tp eoi e
 Z-nimsll íeyeNa Z m ěěu ímdn hoeáp l opte ioe
 -Zinsmll eíeyaNZ m é uě í dm nh eopá lpoeti eo
- iZsnlm le eíayZNm é u ěí d mhne po á pleoite o
-i sZln mele aíZymN é u íěd hmenp o á p elioet o
i-s lZ nemela Zímy Né u í dě h empn o áp e ileo to
is-l ZenemalZ mí yéNu í d ěh e pm n opáe i el oot
sil- eZenamZlm íéyuN í d hěe p m n poeái e loo t
sli -e eZanZmml éíuy Ní d h eěp m np eoiáe ol ot
ls ie-e aZZnmm lé uí yíNd h e pě mpne ioeá o lto
l seie-a ZZmn mélu ííydN h e p ě pmeni eo áo tlo
 leseia-Z mZ némul íídy nh e p ě p emine ooá t ol
 elesaiZ-m Zénem lí dí yhNe p ěp e imen oo át o l
e elasZim- éZun míld íhyeNp pěe i em no otáo l
ee alZsmi -é uZ nímdl híeypN p eěi e mon tooál
eea Zlms ié-u Zíndm lh eípy N p e iěe om nt oolá
eaeZ ml séiu- íZdn mhle pí y N p e i eě o mtno lo á
aeZem lésui -í dZ nhmelp í y Np e i e ěo tmonl o á
aZeme élus ií-d Zhnempl í ypNe i e oě t omln oá
Zame eé ul síid- hZenpm l ípyeNi e o ět o lm n áo
Zma eéeu lísdi -h eZpn m l píeyiNe o těo l m ná o
mZ aéeue ílds ih-e pZ n m lp eíiyeN o t oěl máno
m Zéaue eí dl shie-p Z n mple iíey No t o lě ámon
 méZua eíed lhseip- Z npmeli eí yoN t o l ě á om n
 émuZ aíede hlespi - Zpnemile íoy Nt o l ěá o mn
é um Zíade eh elps i - pZenimel oí ytNo l áěo nm
éu míZda ehee pl s i -p eZinem lo ítyoNl á oě n m
ué ímdZ aheeep l s ip-e iZen mol tíoylN á o ěn m
u éí dm Zhaeepe l spie-i eZ nom lt oíly N á o něm
 uíéd mhZeape e lpseii-e Zon mtlo lí i y Ná o n mě
 íudé hmeZpa e e plesiie- oZ ntmoll í yáNo n m ě
í du éh empZ a e ep elisei -o Ztnomll íáyoN n m ě
íd uhée pm Z a epee iles io- tZonlm l áíoy Nn m ě
dí hueép m Z apeeei el soi -t oZln m lá oí ynNm ě
d íh eupé m Zpaeeiee los it-o lZ n málo ínymN ě
 dhíe pu é mpZeaieee ol stio-l Z námol nímy N ě
 hdeíp u é pmeZiaee eo ltsoil- Zánom ln mí y Ně
h edpí u ép emiZea eoe tlosli - áZon mnlm í yěN
he pd í upée imeZ aoe et olls i -á oZ nnmml íěy N
ehp d í pueéi em Zoa eteo ll s iá-o Znnmm l ěí y N
eph d íp euiée moZ ateoel l sáio- nZmn m lě í y N
pe h dpíe iueé om Ztaoele lásoi -n mZ n měl í y N
p e h pdeíi eu éo mtZoale e álos in-m Z něm l í yN
 p e hp ediíe uoé tmoZla e eá ol snim- Zěn m l íNy
 p ephe ideí ou ét omlZ a eáeo lnsmi - ěZ n m l Níy
 ppeehi ed ío utéo lm Z aáeoe nlms i -ě Z n m lN yí
 ppeeihe doí tuoél m Záaoe en ml s iě- Z n mNly í
 p epieeh od ít oulé máZoa enem l sěi - Z nNmylí
 p e ipee ho dtío lu é ámoZ aneme lěs i - ZNnymíl
 pe i ep eoh tdoíl u éá om Zname e ěl s i - NZyním l
 pe i e poe ht odlí uáéo mnZma e eě l s i -N yZín ml
 epi e op etho ld í áuoé nmmZ a eěe l s iN-y íZ nlm
 eipe o pteohl d íá ou én mm Z aěe e l sNiy-í Zlnm
 ieep o tpoelh dáío uném m Zěa e e lNsyií- lZmn
 iee po t ople h ádoí numé měZ a e e Nlysíi -l mZn
 ei eop t o lp e há od ín mu é ěm Z a e eN ylís il-m nZ

Znám-li síly Nebe a Země mé umění dosáhne plnosti poesie
Zán-mils lí yeNeba Z me ěému ěmínd soháenp nlsoitp eoise
áZ-nimsll íeyeNabZ m eěěumě ímdns hoeápnn sliopte ioes
á-Zinsmll eíeyaNZbm ěeuěěmí dmsnh eopánns ilpoeti eos
-áíZsnlm le eíayZNmb é ueěěímd smhne ponásni pleoite so
-iásZln mele aíZymN bé u ěeíědms hmenp nosáinp elioets o
i-sálZ nemela Zímy Nébu ě íeděsmh empnn soiápne ileosto
is-lá ZenemalZ mí yéNubě í deséhme pmnns iopáeni elsoot
sil- áeZenamZlm íéyuNěbí d sehěemp nmsni poeáine sloo t
sli -éáeZanZmml éíuyěNíbd s heeěpmn sminp eoiáens ol ot
ls ie-eáaZZnmm lé uíěyíNdbs h eepěnms impne ioeásno lto
l seie-aáZZmn mélu ěííydNsbh e peněsmi pmeni eosáon tlo
 leseia-ZámZ némulě íídysNhbe p neseěimp emine sooá nt ol
elesaiZ-má Zénumělí dísyhNebp n seiěpme imens oo átno l
e elasZim- áéZuněmíld síhyeNpbn s iepěemi emsno otáonl
ee alZsmi -éáuZěnímdls híeypNnbs i peeěime smon tooáln
eea Zlms ié-uáěZíndmslh eípynNsbi p eeiěems om nt oolá n
eaeZ ml séiu-ěáíZdnsmhle pínysNibp e ieeěsmo mtno lo án
aeZem lésuiě-íádZsnhmelp nísyiNpbe i eesěom tmonl oná
aZeme élusěíí-dásZhnempln sííypNebi e seoě mt omln noá
Zame eé ulěsíid-sáhZenpmnls iípyeNibe s oe ětmo lm nn áo
Zma eéeu ělísdis-háeZpnnmsli píeyiNebs o etěoml mnná o
mZ aéeueě íldssih-eápZnnsmilp eííyeNsbo teoělm nmáno
m Zéaueěí dlsshie-pánZsnimple iíeysNob t oelě mn ámon
méZuaěeíed slhseip-násZinpmeli eísyoN bt o le ěnmá om n
émuZěaíedes hlespin-sáíZpnemile síoy Ntbo l eněámo mn
é uměZíaedeseh elpsnis-iápZenimels oí ytNobl neáěom nm
éu ěmíZdasehee plnssii-páeZinemslo ítyoNlb n áeoě mn m
uěě ímdZsaheeep nlssiip-eáíZensmol tíoylN bn á oe ěnmm
uěéí dmsZhaeepen slispie-iáeZsnom lt oíly Nnbá o eněmm
ěuíéd smhZeapenes ilpseii-eásZon mtlo lí ynNábo nemě m
ěíudés hmeZpanesei plesiie-sáoZ ntmoll ínyáNob n me ěm
íěduséh empZnaseiep eliseis-oá Ztnomll níáyoN bn m emě
íděsuhée pmnZsaiepee ilessio- átZonlm ln áíoy Nnbm meě
díseěhueép nmsZiapeeei elssoi -táoZln mnlá oí ynNmb m ěe
dsíhěeupén smiZpaeeiee slos it-oálZ nnmálo ínymN bm ě e
sdhíeěpunés impZeaieees ol stio-lá Znnámol nímy Nmbě e
shdeípěnuséí pmeZiaeeseo ltsôil- ánZánom ln mí ymNěbe
hsedpíněsuiép emiZeaseoe tlosli -nááZon mnlm ímyěNeb
hespdníséiupée imeZsaoe et olls in-ááoZ nnmml míěyeN b
ehpsndsííěpueéí emsZoa eteo ll sniá-oá Znnmm lm ěíey N b
ephnssdiíípěeuiée smoZ ateoel lnsáio- ánZmn mmlě eí y Nb
penhssidpíeěiueés om Ztaoele nlásoi -námZ nmměle í ybN
pneshispdeíiěeuséo mtZoale en álos in-má Zmněmel íbyN
npseihpsediíeěsuoé tmoZla eneá ol snim- ámZěnem l bíNy
nspiephesideíséěou ét omlZ aneáeo lnsmi -máéZen m lb Níy
snippeehisedsíoě utéo lm Znaéeoe nlms im-ěáeZ n mblN yí
sinpeeihessdoí ětuoél mnZáaoe en ml smiě-eá Z nbmNly í
ispnepieehssod ítěoulé nmáZoa enem lmsěie- á ZbnNmylí
ipsenipeeshos dtíoělu én ámoZ aneme mlěsei - ábZNnymíl
píesinepseoh stdoílě unéá om Zname em ěles i -báNZyním l
peiisenspoe htsodlí ěnuáéo mnZma emeě el s ib-NáyZín ml
epiiessnop ethosld íněáuoé nmmZ ameěee l sbiN-yáíZ nlm
eipeisson pteohls dníáěou én mm Zmaěeee lbsNiy-íá Zlnm
ieepsios ntpoelh sndáíoě uném mmZěaee e blNsyií- álZmn
ieespoi stnople hnsáóoí ěnumé mměZea e ab Nlysíí -lámZn
eiseop itsonlp enhásod íněmu ém ěmeZ a ebeN ylís il-mánZ

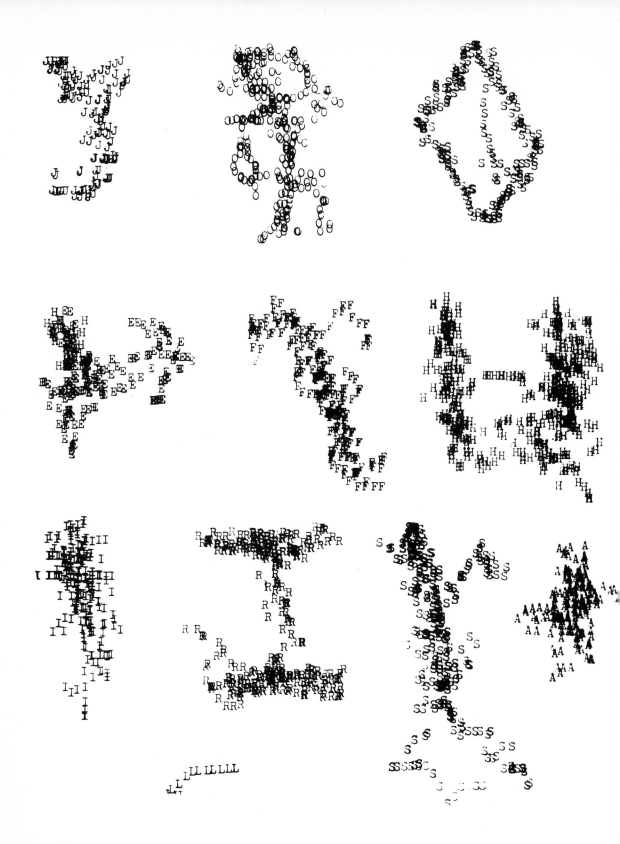

138   Letter typogram (*Buchstabentypogram*)   Josef Honys (mid-1960s)

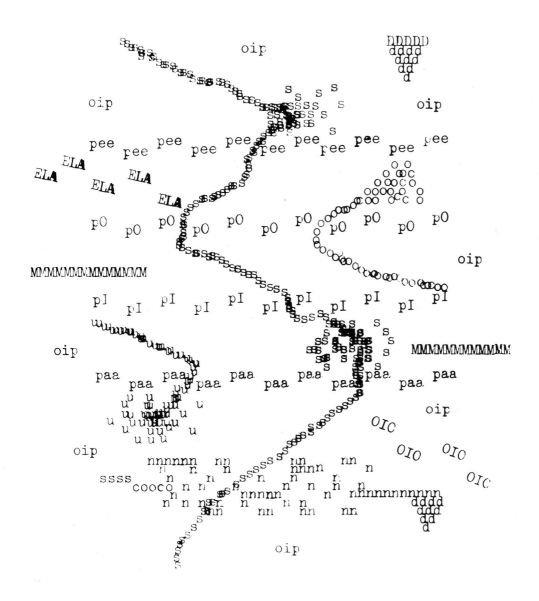

5th dolphin transmission   Andrew Lloyd (1967)

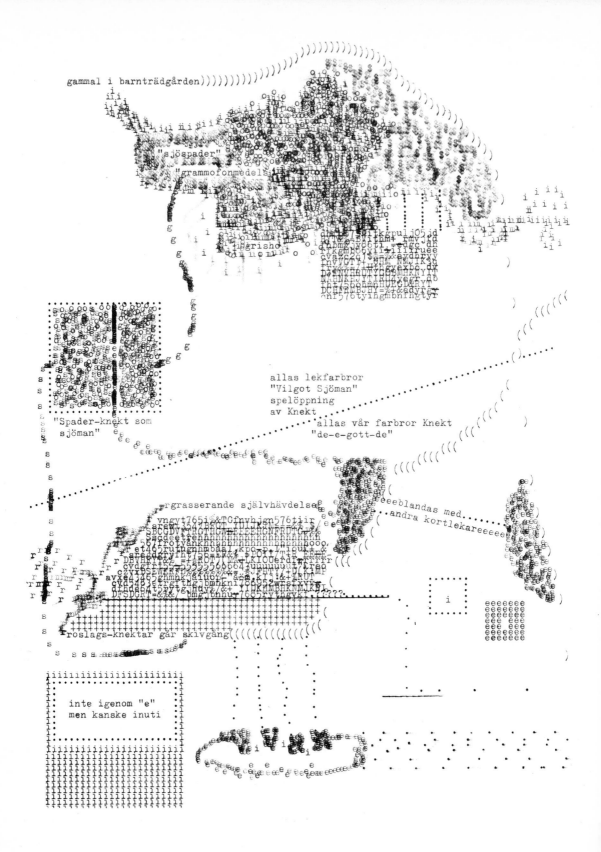

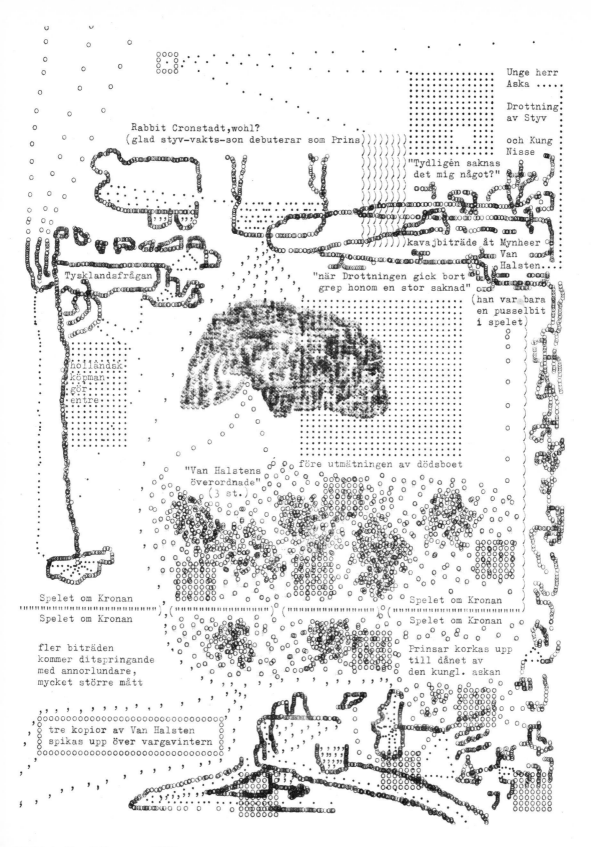

Untitled   Mats G. Bengtsson (1964)

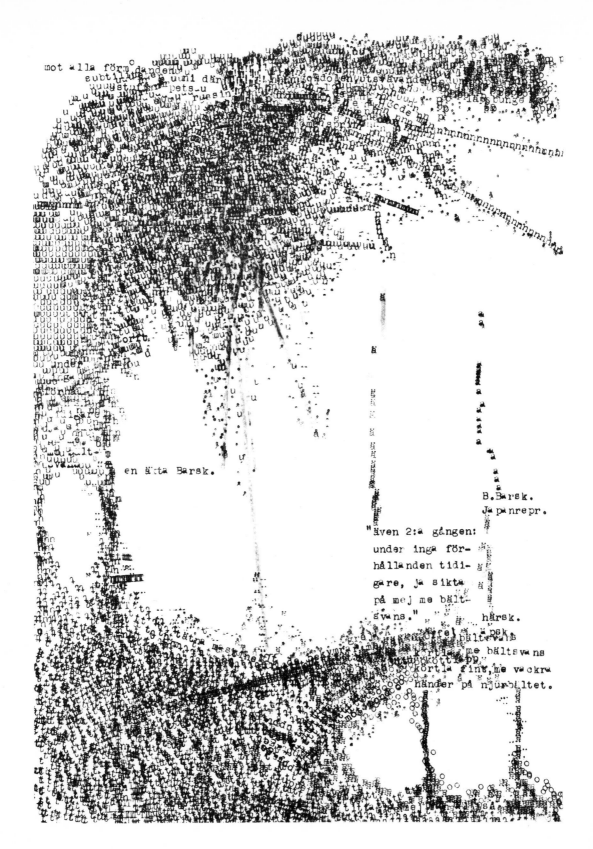

142   Untitled   Bengt Emil Johnson (1963)

Homage to John Cage   Bengt Emil Johnson (1962)

144   Water land   Shohachirō Takahashi (1969)

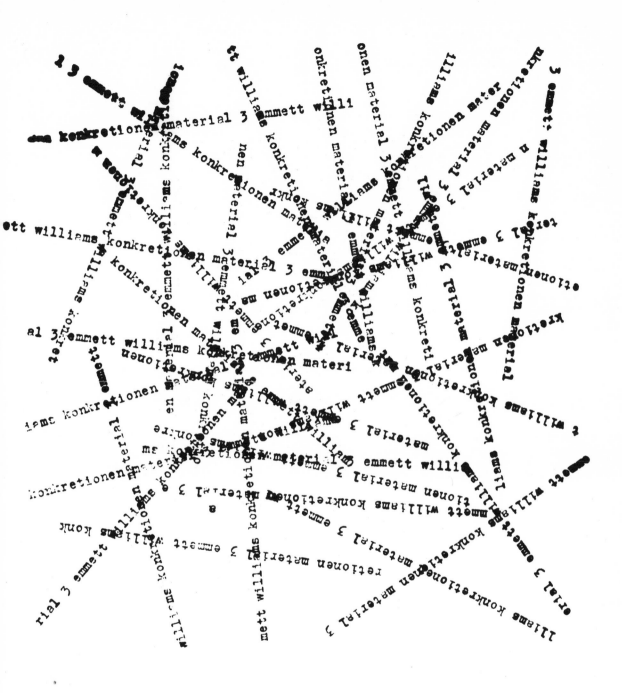

Prospectus for magazine Material   Emmett Williams (1958)

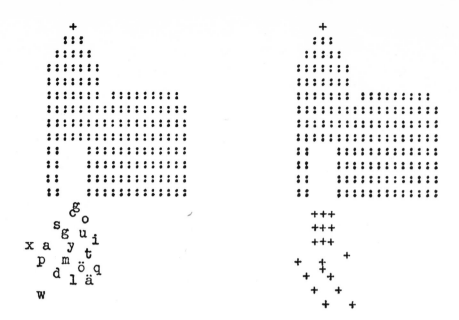

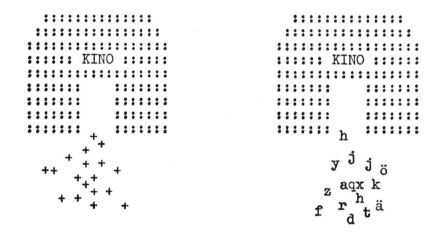

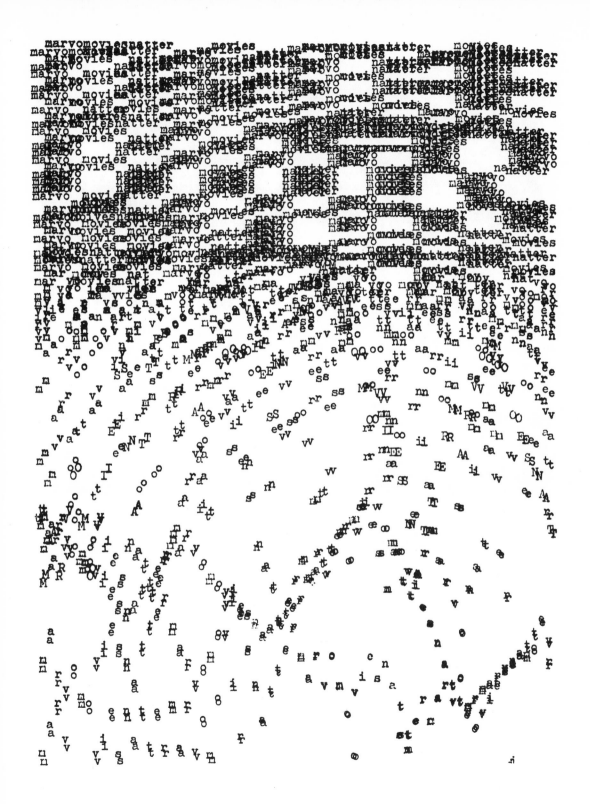

Whisper piece   Bob Cobbing (1969)

148   Beethoven today   Bob Cobbing (1970)

Some relevant books

For those wishing to increase their knowledge of type-writer art, and the wider area in which it relates to concrete poetry and other verbal/visual experiments, the following books may be of interest:

H. N. Werkman. Edited by Fridolin Müller, with an Introduction by Peter F. Althaus and a Biography by Jan Martinet (Verlag Arthur Niggli, 1967).

An Anthology of Concrete Poetry. Edited by Emmett Williams (Something Else Press, 1967).

Concrete Poetry: an international anthology. Edited and with an Introduction by Stephen Bann (London Magazine Editions, 1967).

Concrete Poetry: a World View. Edited and with an Introduction by Mary Ellen Solt (Indiana University Press, 1968).

anthology of concretism. Edited by Eugene Wildman (Swallow Press, 1968).

Pioneers of Modern Typography. Edited and with an Introduction by Herbert Spencer (Lund Humphries, 1969).

The Word as Image. Edited and with an Introduction by Berjoui Bowler (Studio Vista, 1970).

Imaged Words & Worded Images. Edited and with an Introduction by Richard Kostelanetz (Outerbridge & Dienstfrey, 1970).

Mindplay. Edited and with an Introduction by John J. Sharkey (Lorrimer Publishing, 1971).

konkrete poesie. (German-speaking authors only.) Edited by Eugen Gomringer (Philip Reclam Jun., 1972).

Typewriter Poems. Edited by Peter Finch (Second Aeon Publications and Something Else Press, 1972).

Text-Bilder. Edited by Klaus Peter Dencker (M. DuMont Schauberg, 1972)

Breakthrough Fictioneers. Edited and with an Introduction by Richard Kostelanetz (Something Else Press, 1973).

Biographical notes

Adler, Jeremy; born 1947 in London. Lecturer, Westfield College (London University). Began calligraphic texts 1967, thereafter typewriter and stencil graphics. Exhibited at Elvaston Gallery, London, Bristol Arts Centre, Goldsmiths' College. Published in Poetry Review, London Magazine, British Book News, Kroklok, Kontexts, Typewriter, etc. Publications: *Alphabox,* 1973 (Writers Forum); *Tarot Cards,* 1973 (Pirate Press); *Alphabet Music,* 1974 (Alphabox, Pirate Press and Writers Forum). Editor of *A,* an envelope magazine of visual poetry.

Bain, Willard S.; born 1938 in San Antonio, Texas. After graduating from Reed College, Portland, Oregon, in 1960, worked three and a half years as a newsman for the San Francisco Bureau of the Associated Press. Wrote teleprinter novel, *Informed Sources,* published in America 1967 and in Britain 1970 (Faber).

Barborka, Zdeněk; born 1938 in Rokycany, Czechoslovakia. Studied music in Pilsen, and became music teacher. Now editor of music programmes for Czech Radio. Published traditional poetry 1957–64, since then experimenting with a series of 'textes processuels'. Contributor to anthology *Concrete Poetry: a World View.* Publications: *Textes processuels* and *Les textes pour la méditation.*

Belsey, Andrew; born 1942 in Huntingdonshire, England. Lecturer in Philosophy at University College, Cardiff. Contributor to London Magazine and other reviews. Publications: five *Converse* postcards (concrete poetry) and *Anaximander,* a collection of traditional poetry, 1974 (Outposts Publications).

Bengtsson, Mats G.; born in Sweden. Musician as well as sound and visual poet. Pioneered visual poetry in Sweden with Bengt Emil Johnson. Publication: *Nutcracker,* 1964 (Albert Bonniers Förlag).

Blake, Gary; born 1943 in Wellington, New Zealand. Studied graphic design at Royal College of Art, London, and with partner now runs a small design group in London specialising in film and print communication.

Bremer, Claus; born 1924 in Hamburg. Theatre director as well as playwright and poet. Lives in Zürich, where two of his plays have been performed, *Dichter Unbekannt,* 1972, and *Hier wird Geld verdient,* 1973. He has been a dramaturg at Darmstadt, Bern, Ulm, Düsseldorf and Zürich, and translated Aeschylus, Aristophanes, Audiberti, Gatti, Grumberg, Ionesco, Prévert, Shakespeare, Sophocles, Spoerri, Tzara and Vitez. Publications include: *Poesie,* 1960; *Ideogramme,* 1964; *Engagierende Texte,* 1966; *Texte und Kommentare,* 1968; *Anlässe,* 1970.

Bridgwater, Patrick; born 1931 in England. Lecturer in German at Leicester University. Contributor to Apollinaire exhibition at Institute of Contemporary Arts in London in 1968. Had one-man exhibition of 'Typograms' at Leicester College of Art, 1968. Work published in anthologies *Imaged Words & Worded Images* and *Mindplay.*

Caldwell, Robert; born 1946 in Whittier, California. Founder and editor of Typewriter, a review started in 1971 specialising in typewriter works, though not exclusively (Post Office Box 409, Iowa City, Iowa 52240 USA). His work here was published in Typewriter. Made wood and plastic wood structures 1970–72. Publications: *15*, 1973 (Bird in the Bush) and *Wands*, an animated field poem with Kent Zimmerman, 1973 (Bird in the Bush).

Cameron, Charles. Born in England but now lives in United States, where he edits a magazine. Organised second British international concrete poetry exhibition while still a student at Oxford in 1965. Published in anthology *The Word as Image*.

Chopin, Henri; born 1922 in Paris. Founded Cinquième Saison, a review for concrete poetry and theoretical texts for sound poetry, in 1958. Founded review OU in 1964. Has pioneered use of throat microphone in sound poetry since 1955. Moved to England in 1968. Retrospective one-man shows at Sunderland Arts Centre in 1972 and Whitechapel Art Gallery, London, in 1974. Publications include: *Signes*, 1957; *l'Arrivista*, 1958; *La Crevette Amoureuse*, 1967; *Le Dernier Roman du Monde*, 1970; *Le Cimetière*, 1971. Record: *Audiopoems*, 1974 (Tangent TGS106).

Cinicolo, Donato; born 1948 in San Bartolomeo, southern Italy. Has lived in England since 1956. Trained as a mechanical engineer, then studied graphics at Watford and St Martin's schools of art. Now with an environmental design consortium. Works published in various magazines, including Typewriter. His typewriter cityscape here was commissioned by Calder & Boyars as a cover design for Alain Robbe-Grillet's novel *Project for a Revolution in New York*.

Claire, Paula; born 1939 in Northampton, England. Writes sound and visual poetry, performs in Britain and abroad, often with audience participation. Besides poems in glass in conjunction with husband, stained-glass artist Paul San Casciani, recent work includes scorch-mark poems, first exhibited at the Europalia exhibition, Belgium, 1974, and pieces with stone shapes and textures. Publications: *Soundsword*, 1972 (Writers Forum); *S-tones improvisation text-ures*, 1974 (Writers Forum).

Clavin, Hans; born 1946 in Ijmuiden, Holland. Founder, 1970, and editor of magazine Subvers. His concrete poetry has been exhibited in group shows in Europe and South America. Publications: *L'histoire de l'histoire*, 1968; *Open het woord*, 1968; *Holland var. 969*, 1970 (De Tafelronde), $\frac{porno}{graphic}$ poetry, 1971 (Subvers) and *L'angerie*, 1973 (De Bezige bij Amsterdam).

Cobbing, Bob; born 1920 in Enfield, England. Co-editor and publisher of Writers Forum Poets and founder, with Peter Mayer, in 1968 of Westminster Group (WOUP) of experimental poets. Co-editor with Dom Sylvester Houédard of sound poetry magazine Kroklok. Began his career as a painter, but has been experimenting with typewriter and mimeographed typewriter works since 1942, and sound poems since 1963. Organised seventh international sound poetry festival at National Poetry Centre, London, in 1974. Has made several sound poetry records, including one with Ernst Jandl. Publications include: *Sound Poems*, 1965; *Eyearun*, 1966; *Kurrirrurriri*,

1967, and *Sonic Icons*, 1970 (all Writers Forum). As editor: *GLOUP and WOUP*, 1974 (Arc Publications).

Collins, Dennis W. A.; born 1912 at Sutton Coldfield, England. Began career as commercial artist in Birmingham. Moved to advertising agency in Liverpool in 1933. After Second World War went freelance, and nine years later began drawing strip cartoons. Since 1958 has drawn 'The Perishers' for the Daily Mirror. Has exhibited drawings and paintings with the Wirral Society of Arts. Writes some poetry.

Dencker, Klaus Peter; born 1941 in Lübeck, Germany. Poet, artist and television film-maker. Works in film and TV department at university of Erlangen-Nürnberg. Won cultural prize of city of Erlangen, 1972, and prize of the German Foreign Office, 1974. Makes visual poetry on paper and film and room events and communications situations. Compiled *Text-Bilder*, an anthology of visual poetry past and present, 1972 (M. DuMont Schauberg).

de Saga, Pietro. This was the pseudonym of Stefi Kiesler, wife of the Austrian architect Friedrich Kiesler, who experimented with the typewriter at the same time as H. N. Werkman was working in Holland and Josef Albers was using the typewriter in his course at the Bauhaus in Germany. She may have been associated with the Bauhaus, as her work was published in its magazine in the 1920s. She emigrated to America, where she is believed to have died.

de Vree, Paul; born 1909 in Antwerp, Belgium. Teacher, poet, painter, film-maker, critic. Founder and director of review De Tafelronde and co-founder of review Lotta Poetica. Several one-man shows, including at Studio Santandrea, Milan, 1972, and Studio Brescia, Brescia, 1973, 1974. Publications include: *Explositieven*, 1966; *Poëzie in fusie*, 1968; *Zimprovisaties*, 1968; *Verbaal gelaat*, 1970; *Poëzien*, 1971; *Poëvisiva*, 1974.

Döhl, Reinhard; born 1934 in Stuttgart, Germany. Assistant at the Institute of Literature and Linguistics at University of Stuttgart. Many visual poems published in book and pamphlet form since *Il Texte*, 1960; among them *Je m'en fiche*, 1961; *Apfel/Wurm*, 1965; *Geht geht und geht*, 1967; *Man*, 1968.

Edmonds, Tom; 1944–71. Born at Aylesford, England. One of the finest English concrete poets and artists, whose work was achieving wide acclaim in the years immediately before his death at twenty-seven. Won Biddulph Scholarship, 1965. Was part-time teacher at Leicester and Chelsea schools of art. Made glass box constructions using receding layers of letters. Posthumous show of these and his 'type tracks' at Serpentine Gallery, London, in 1972.

Etlinger, Amelia; born 1933 in New York. Makes 'hanging poem' objects, in some of which abstract patterns are typed on to silk. Organised concrete poetry exhibition at Harmanus Bleecker Library, New York, 1971. Typewriter works published in De Tafelronde and Kontexts.

Fareed, Iqbal; born 1941 in Mysore, India. Worked for twelve years in the Police Department but is now a calligrapher in Urdu at the Central Institute of Indian Languages, Mysore. A poet of Urdu 'gazals', his work has been published in Government and private magazines and collections. His typewriter portraits have won wide acclaim in India.

Federman, Raymond; born 1928 in France. Professor of French and Comparative Literature at State University of New York at Buffalo. Apart from works in literary reviews (Adam, London; Panache, Chicago), he has appeared in anthologies *Breakthrough Fictioneers* and *Imaged Words & Worded Images*. Has published two bilingual (French/English) poetry collections, two books on Samuel Beckett, and a typewriter novel, *Double or Nothing*, 1971 (Swallow Press).

Ferro, Luigi; born 1931 at Vercelli, Italy. In 1967 he produced two series of concrete texts – 'Chromatic permutations' and 'Iconograms' – using photo-mechanical overlay techniques. Since then he has experimented with three-dimensional modular forms. In 1968, he put on a 'spatial game event' with modules, in which the public was asked to participate, at Fiumalbo, Anfo and Novara. Has exhibited in many international group shows. One-man shows: Gallery Ten, London, 1968; Centro documentazione visiva, Piacenza, 1968; Galleria Sincron, Brescia, 1969; Le Disque Rouge, Brussels, 1969; Rassegna S. Fedele 1, Milan, 1971 and Rassegna S. Fedele 2, Centro ti. zero, Turin, 1972. Publications: *moltiplicazione* (Geiger, Turin); *itineraire* (Agentzia, Paris) and *tong*, 1974 (Geiger, Turin).

Finch, Peter; born 1947 in Cardiff. Editor of Second Aeon Publications. Manages the Welsh Arts Council's Cardiff bookshop, Oriel. Won Welsh Arts Council experimental poetry bursary 1969–70. Edited anthology *Typewriter Poems*, 1972 (Second Aeon and Something Else Press). Has published ten books and pamphlets of poetry, including work in the traditional field.

Garnier, Ilse; born 1927 in Kaiserslautern, Germany. Collaborator, in many works, with husband Pierre.

Garnier, Pierre; born 1928 in Amiens, France. Editor since 1963 of spatialist review Les Lettres. Publications include: *Les Armes de la Terre*, 1954 (André Silvaire); *Seconde Géographie*, 1959 (Gallimard); *Prototypes*, 1964 (Silvaire); *Poèmes franco-japonais*, 1966, with Seiichi Niikuni (Silvaire); *Spatialisme et Poésie Concrète*, 1968 (Gallimard), and *Esquisses Palatines*, 1972 (Silvaire); and a record, made with Ilse Garnier and Seiichi Niikuni, *Textes sur Spatialisme*, 1972 (Columbia Records, Japan).

Gibbs, Michael; born 1949 in England. Editor of visual poetry magazine Kontexts. Has exhibited in several group shows. One-man exhibition at In-Out Center, Amsterdam, 1974. Included in anthologies *Mindplay* and *Typewriter Poems*. Publications: *Life Line*, 1972 (Kontexts) and *Connotations*, 1973 (Second Aeon).

Gray Hulse, Tristan; born in Cheshire, England. Became interested in visual poetry through the works of Diter Rot and Dom Sylvester Houédard. Published 'Logograms' (concrete haiku) in Haiku Byways: 5, winter 1972–73.

Greer, Robin. Lives in London, where he was active in concrete poetry movement in mid-1960s, specialising in typewriter works. Contributor to anthology *The Word as Image*.

Havel, Václav; born 1936 in Prague. Resident playwright at Theatre of the Balustrade in Prague. Has had two plays performed, *The Garden Party* and *Memorandum*. Contributor to anthologies *Concrete Poetry: a World View* and *An Anthology of Concrete Poetry*. Publications include *The Anticodes* – typographical poems.

Hiršal, Josef; born 1920 in Chomutičky, Czechoslovakia. Translator, poet, teacher, journalist, editor. Co-editor with B. Grögerova of anthology *Poezie experimentálni*, 1968. Included in folder of Czechoslovak concrete poetry published by the Stedelijk Museum, Amsterdam, in 1970. Contributor to anthologies *Concrete Poetry: a World View* and *anthology of concretism*. Publications include: *Slovo, pismo, akce, hlas*, 1967, and *Job Boj*, 1968 (both with B. Grögerova).

Hollis, Will; 1893–1973. For fifty years librarian to the Imperial Typewriter Co. in Leicester, Will Hollis perfected his photographic style of typewriter portraiture in the years following the Second World War. It is not known whether he ever saw Dennis Collins' similar efforts. He died early in 1973, without knowing that his works – which he called 'callitypes' – were about to be exhibited for the first time, at the Typewriter Art exhibition at the New 57 Gallery in Edinburgh in November.

Honys, Josef; 1919–69. Born in Jičin, Czechoslovakia. Artist as well as poet. Included in folder of Czechoslovak concrete poetry published by the Stedelijk Museum, Amsterdam, in 1970.

Houédard, Dom Sylvester; born 1924 in Guernsey, Channel Islands. Has been Benedictine monk at Prinknash Abbey, Gloucester, since 1949. Was a prominent figure in introducing concrete poetry to Britain in 1961, and since then has become its leading theorist as well as an outstanding practitioner. Is co-editor, with Bob Cobbing, of sound poetry review Kroklok. His typewriter compositions (which he calls 'typestracts') have been exhibited all over the world and he has had one-man shows at the Lisson Gallery, London, in the late 1960s, at the Victoria and Albert Museum, London, in 1971, and at the Laing Art Gallery, Newcastle, in 1972. His work has not yet appeared in book form, but among his pamphlets are: *Kinkon*, 1965, and *Tantric Poems Perhaps*, 1966 (both Writers Forum).

Jandl, Ernst; born 1925 in Vienna. Teaches at grammar schools there. Has been experimenting with new forms of poetry since mid-1950s. One of the most successful sound poets, he established himself – and perhaps sound poetry in general – at the Albert Hall poetry festival, London, in 1966. His visually oriented typewriter works are only marginal to his main effort in the sound and concrete field. Publications include: *Andere Augen*, 1956 (Bergland Verlag); *klare gerührt*, 1964 (Eugen Gomringer); *mai hart lieb zapfen eibe hold*, 1965 (Writers Forum); *Laut und Luise*, 1966 (Walter Verlag); *Sprechblasen*, 1970, and *Der Künstliche Baum*, 1970 (both Hermann Luchterhand).

Johnson, Bengt Emil; born 1936 in Saxdalen, Sweden. Worked there as a shopkeeper till 1965, then moved to Stockholm, where he works in the music department of Swedish Radio. Pianist and composer as well as visual and sound poet. In early 1960s produced series of expressionistic typewriter picture poems and since then has written sound poems for radio and stage performance. Organiser of first six international sound poetry festivals held in Stockholm in conjunction with Swedish Radio. Publications include: *Hyllningarna*, 1963; *Essaer om Bror Barsk och andra dikter*, 1964 (Albert Bonniers Förlag); *Gubbdrunkning*, 1965; *Semikolon* (with Lars-Gunnar Bodin), 1966.

Kern, W. Bliem; born 1943 in Philadelphia. Artist as well as sound and visual poet. First prize in sculpture and painting show at Avanti Gallery, New York, 1969. Director and founder of Sound Poetry Workshop, to find new forms in poetry. Publication: sound and visual sequence *Meditationsmeditationsmeditations*, 1974 (New Rivers Press).

Kolář, Jiří; born 1914 in Protivin, Czechoslovakia. One of the most prominent figures in the Czech avant-garde. Worked as a joiner, labourer and waiter before becoming a writer in 1943. In late 1940s became member of artists' group 42. Editor of Prague publishing house of Dilo, 1945–48. One-man shows of his collages in London, Genoa, Vienna, Miami and elsewhere. Has written two plays, *Pest in Atheñ*, 1965, and *Unser täglich Brot*, 1966. Contributor to anthologies *Concrete Poetry: a World View, An Anthology of Concrete Poetry*, and *Text-Bilder*. Publications include: *Hommage an K. Malevich*, 1959; *Y 61*, 1960; *Evidente Gedichte*, 1965; *Der Aesop aus Werschowitz*, 1966.

Kostelanetz, Richard: born 1940 in New York. Has edited numerous anthologies, among them *Imaged Words & Worded Images*, 1970 (Outerbridge & Dienstfrey) and *Breakthrough Fictioneers*, 1973 (Something Else Press). His other publications include: poetry – *Visual Language*, 1970 (Assembling Press); criticism – *The Theatre of Mixed Means*, 1968 (Dial Press), and *Metamorphosis in the Arts*, 1972 (Abrams); and autobiography – *Recycling*, 1974 (Assembling). As editor: *John Cage*, 1974 (W. H. Allen).

Lloyd, Andrew; born 1943 in Surrey, England. Contributor to Kontexts and anthologies *Mindplay* and *Typewriter Poems*. Publication: *The Quietest Ice* (Vertigo).

Lora-Totino, Arrigo; born 1928 in Turin. Founded experimental review antipiugiù in 1960, and modulo, 1966, first number of which was an international anthology of concrete poetry. His paintings, and poems in plexiglass, have been widely exhibited since his first one-man show in Milan in 1959. A series of his chromatic typewriting texts was published in De Tafelronde, 1967. He set up, with Carlo Belloli, the Museum of Contemporary Poetry at Turin. Organised concrete poetry exhibition at Venice Biennale 1969. His sound poetry, *Phonemes*, was published on disc by Franz Mon, 1971 (at Neuwied am Rhein), and by Source, 1971 (issue no. 9, Sacramento, California).

McCaffery, Steve; born 1947 in Barnsley, England, but has lived in Toronto since 1968. He has been experimenting with language disintegration/reintegration both sonically and visually since 1966. Has exhibited at the Stedelijk Museum, Amsterdam, and in Stuttgart, Paris and London. He is co-editor of Gronk, co-founder of the Toronto Research Group (with B. P. Nichol) and a member of the sound poetry ensemble The Four Horsemen. Publications: *Ground Plans for a Speaking City*, 1970 (Anonbeyond Press); *Transitions to the Beast*, 1970 (Ganglia Press); *maps: a different landscape*, 1972 (Ganglia/Gronk); *Carnival: first panel 1967–70*, 1973 (Coach House Press); *O'ws Waif*, 1973 (Coach House Press); *Louis Riel:*

a legend, 1973 (Massassauga Editions).

McDonough, Tim; born 1949 in Saginaw, Michigan. Works in publishing in New York. Has recently experimented with audience participation sound poems and has written a series of nature poems with Magic Marker on 30-by-40-inch posterboard. In 1973 published a small-scale version of 'Cityscape Modular Mural Poem' in *Assembling*, and gave reading of 'Phive' (all the five-letter words in the *Random House Dictionary of the English Language*) at the Tenth Annual Avant Garde Art Festival in New York. A selection of his poems appeared in Typewriter in 1974.

Mayer, Peter; born 1935 in Berlin. Teaches visual communication at Goldsmiths' College (London University). Co-founder, with Bob Cobbing, in 1968 of Westminster Group (WOUP) of experimental poets. Makes 3D/film poems. Has lectured on visual poetry at Institute of Contemporary Arts and National Poetry Centre, London. Showed in Europalia exhibition, Belgium 1974. Magazine contributions include analytical and critical articles in Poetry Review and Journal of Typographical Research. Represented in anthologies *Mindplay* and *Typewriter Poems*. Publications: 'Yin Yang' cube, 1968; *Gamme de gamma*, 1970; *Earmouth*, 1972.

Morgan, Robert; born 1930 in New York. Now lives in London, where he works as a lecturer in film production at the London College of Printing. Is also a film director – mainly of television documentaries – and a freelance graphic designer. His contribution here is part of his design for the sleeve of Henri Chopin's record *Audiopoems*.

Nannucci, Maurizio; born 1939 in Florence. As well as exhibiting throughout Europe in group shows since 1961, he has had 17 one-man shows between his first, at the gallery La Cimaise in Brest in 1965, and his neon works at the Salone Annunciata in Milan in 1973. Member of the group of the Studio di Musica elettronica S 2 F M, in Florence. Has made object poems, books, multiples, and researched into the applications of the computer in the visual and musical field.

Niikuni, Seiichi; born 1925 in Sendai, Japan. Founder and editor of magazine for concrete poetry and spatialism, Asa, 1964. Since then his concrete poetry has been exhibited and anthologised in Europe and America. In mid-1960s, while living in Paris, collaborated with Pierre Garnier in producing *Poèmes franco-japonais*, a series of visual texts which combine passages typed on Japanese with those on Western typewriters. One-man show at Whitechapel Gallery, London, in 1974. Contributor to anthologies *Concrete Poetry: a World View, An Anthology of Concrete Poetry* and anthology of concretism. Publications include: *Zero. On*, 1963; *Fonetisch - en klanggedicht Entrance*, 1965; *Mer* (with Ilse Garnier), 1966; *Lips and jealousy*, 1970.

Parritt, Simon; born 1950 in Wimbledon, London. Studied at Croydon art school and Goldsmiths' College. Exhibited typewriter works at Wiggins Teape, London, and Goldsmiths' College in 1973. Works published in Microphone (cover) and A, both in 1972. Publication: *Zeotrope*, 1974.

Pazarkaya, Yüksel; born 1940 in Izmir, Turkey. Lives in Germany. Has written plays for the stage and radio, as well as fiction and poetry (traditional and concrete). Contributor to anthologies *Konkrete Poesie International*, 1966 (Hansjörg Mayer, Stuttgart), and *Text-Bilder*.

Popović, Zoran; born 1944 in Jugoslavia. Lives in Belgrade, where he has exhibited in concrete poetry shows and is a regular contributor to the review Signal. Contributed to Jugoslav event-art performance at Demarco Gallery at Edinburgh Festival, 1973. Published in anthology *Text-Bilder*.

Riddell, Alan; born 1927 in Townsville, Australia. Brought up in Scotland, he founded the poetry review Lines in Edinburgh in 1952. Started as traditional poet but began writing concrete poetry in 1963, after being introduced to the genre by Ian Hamilton Finlay. Published first visual poem in Encounter in 1955. Won Heinemann Prize in Australia in 1956 and Scottish Arts Council Poetry Prize in 1968. One-man concrete show at New 57 Gallery, Edinburgh, in 1971. Publications: *Beneath the Summer*, 1952 (Macdonald, Edinburgh); *Majorcan Interlude*, 1960 (Macdonald, Edinburgh); *The Stopped Landscape*, 1968 (Hutchinson); and *Eclipse*, concrete poems, 1972 (Calder & Boyars).

Shimizu, Toshihiko; born 1929 in Chiba, Japan. Photographer and jazz critic as well as artist and poet. Member of avant-garde artists' group VOU, founded in Tokyo in 1935. Made first 'letter pictures' in 1965, and since then his work has appeared in exhibitions in Japan and overseas, including ? Concrete Poetry organised by the Stedelijk Museum, Amsterdam, in 1970. Contributor to *Text-Bilder*.

Stacey, Flora F. F. Nothing is known of Flora Stacey beyond the fact that in the late 1890s her typewriter drawings were much admired in Britain for their painstaking skill and craftsmanship.

Takahashi, Shohachirō; born 1933 in Japan. Poet and photographer. Member of Japanese avant-garde artists' group VOU. Like his friend Toshihiko Shimizu, has exhibited in many international group shows. One-man shows at Gallery Yamagoa, Kitakami, 1961; Centro Tool, Milan, 1971; Galerie Senatore, Stuttgart, 1971. Publications: *Oiseaux*, 1968; *Vent*, 1968; *Ombre*, 1968; *Terre d'eau terre de feu*, 1969; *Domaine de <a·i>*, 1972.

Themerson, Stefan; born 1910 in Plock, Poland. With wife Franciszka, a painter, made several avant-garde films in Warsaw in the 1930s. Served in the Polish army in France during the Second World War and escaped to England after the fall of France. Since the war has written almost exclusively in English. Publications include: experimental poetry – *Semantic Divertissements*, 1962 (Gaberbocchus Press); novels – *Bayamus*, 1949 (Editions Poetry London), *Cardinal Pölätüo*, 1961, and *Tom Harris*, 1967 (both Gaberbocchus); stories – *Wooff Wooff or Who killed Richard Wagner?*, 1951 (Gaberbocchus); and essays – *factor T*, 1956, *Kurt Schwitters in England*, 1958, and *Apollinaire's Lyrical Ideograms*, 1968 (all Gaberbocchus).

Todorović, Miroljub; born 1940 in Skopje, Jugoslavia. Founder of Signalism, an avant-garde movement, and chief editor of Signal, its magazine. Has exhibited in international group shows and has had one-man shows in Jugoslavia. Publications include: *Planet*, 1965; *Signal*, 1970; *Kyberno*, 1970; *Trip to Starland*, 1971; *The Pig is an excellent Swimmer*, 1971; *Gift Parcel*, 1972; *Certainly Milk Flame Bee*, 1972; *Thirty Signalist Poems*, 1973; *Approaches*, 1973.

Ulrichs, Timm; born 1940 in Berlin. Studied architecture at Hanover, 1959–66. His visual poetry, texts, pictures, objects, films and environments have been shown in Germany and internationally since 1961. He is now producing works of 'total art, idea art, body art, nature art, instant art, *basic art*, placebo art, etc.'. Has had thirty-five one-man shows. Contributor to *anthology of concretism*. Publications include *Klartexte*, 1966; *Spielpläne*, 1969; and *Weiter in Text*, 1969.

Valoch, Jiří; born 1946 in Brno, Czechoslovakia. Works in print room of museum at Brno, where he is also an art critic and theorist. His typewriter works have been widely published in magazines and his objects have been shown in many exhibitions. Publications include: *Tipogrammi, vibrazioni, constellazioni particulare*, 1964; *Meccanici*, 1965; *Poemi ottici II*, 1967; and *Schemi*, 1967.

Ward, J. P.; born 1937 in Felixstowe, England. Lecturer in English at University College, Swansea. Organised Welsh Arts Council concrete poetry exhibition in Cardiff, 1969. Experimental and concrete poetry published in Poetry Review, Time Out, London Magazine, Contrasts, Second Aeon, and in anthology *Typewriter Poems*. Publications: two collections of traditional poetry, *The Other Man* and *The Line of Knowledge* (both Christopher Davies), and folder of concrete, *From Alphabet to Logos*, 1972 (Second Aeon).

Werkman, H. N.; 1882–1945. Born in Leens, Holland. After an early career as a journalist, became a small jobbing printer in the early 1920s in the university town of Groningen. Began to make one-off prints using printers' materials – display types, rules, rollers and so on – as well as his pioneering 'typeprints' on the typewriter. Was murdered by Nazis a few days before the liberation of northern Holland in April 1945. His typographical originality is appraised in Herbert Spencer's *Pioneers of Modern Typography*, 1969 (Lund Humphries), and his art in general in *H. N. Werkman*, 1967 (Verlag Arthur Niggli).

Williams, Emmett; born 1925 in Greenville, South Carolina. From 1946 to 1966 lived in Europe, where he met Claus Bremer and Daniel Spoerri, with both of whom he collaborated in Darmstadt in founding the avant-garde magazine Material, in 1957. This was completely set on typewriters and one of his pieces here was taken from an issue devoted to Williams's own work. Is now chief editor of the Something Else Press, for whom he edited *An Anthology of Concrete Poetry* in 1967. Publications include: *13 Variations on 6 words of Gertrude Stein*, 1965; *Sweethearts*, 1967; and *A Boy and a Bird*, 1969.

Zenker, Helmut; born 1949 in St Valentin, Austria. For two years a schoolteacher, he is now a freelance writer in Vienna and the Tyrol. Since 1968 his visual texts have appeared in various magazines, including Wespennest, Contra, Antiquarium, Neues Forum, Eselsmilch and Auswege. Contributor to anthology *Text-Bilder*. Show of visual texts at Camera Obscura, Vienna, in 1969.

Acknowledgements

For permission to print the works in this book, the following acknowledgements are made:

Jeremy Adler: 'Leaflikebird' from London Magazine and 'Likecityscape' from British Book News, to the author.

Willard S. Bain: Illustration from novel Informed Sources (1970), to Faber & Faber and the author.

Zdeněk Barborka: 'Nine meditations on a theme of Jiří Kolář', to the Stedelijk Museum and the author.

Andrew Belsey: 'Train types' from London Magazine, to the author.

Mats G. Bengtsson: Two pages from Nutcracker (Albert Bonniers Förlag, 1964), to the author.

Gary Blake: 'Typewriter', to the author.

Claus Bremer: 'Lesbares in unlesbares übersetzen' from Concrete Poetry: an international anthology (London Magazine Editions, 1967), 'Dove' from Text-Bilder (M. DuMont Schauberg, 1972) and 'Infantryman', to the author.

Patrick Bridgwater: 'Anatomy of a tomato' from Imaged Words & Worded Images (Outerbridge & Dienstfrey, 1970), to the author.

Robert Caldwell: 'Susan' from Typewriter, to the author.

Charles Cameron: 'Poem for Rosemarie' from The Word as Image (Studio Vista, 1970), to the author.

Henri Chopin: 'Bird' and 'Graphic poem' from Le Dernier Roman du Monde (Ed. Cyanuur, 1970), to the author.

Donato Cinicolo: 'Cityscape', to Calder & Boyars and the author.

Paula Claire: 'Sea shanty' from Soundsword (1972), to Writers Forum and the author.

Hans Clavin: 'luv', to the author.

Bob Cobbing: 'Whisper piece' from The Word as Image (Studio Vista, 1970), to the author; 'Worm' from Kurrirrurriri (1967) and 'Beethoven today' from Sonic Icons (1970), to Writers Forum and the author.

Dennis W. A. Collins: 'Churchill', 'Duke of Edinburgh' and 'Queen Elizabeth', to the author.

Klaus Peter Dencker: 'Announcement', to the author.

Pietro de Saga: 'Composition' from Pioneers of Modern Typography (Lund Humphries, 1969), to Herbert Spencer.

Paul de Vree: Untitled from Explositieven (De Tafelronde, 1966), to the author; 'To Mrs M. Luther King', 'Arise the dead' and 'Life is a lottery' from Zimprovisaties (De Tafelronde, 1968), to the author.

Reinhard Döhl: 'Rauf runter rauf', to the author.

Tom Edmonds: 'Towards me writing a book', to Miss Frances M. Newman and Dr Edmonds.

Amelia Etlinger: Untitled (page 123) from De Tafelronde and cover design from Kontexts, to the author.

Iqbal Fareed: 'Gandhi', to the author.

Raymond Federman: Page from novel Double or Nothing (Swallow Press, 1971), to the author.

Luigi Ferro: 'Chromatic permutations', to the author.

Peter Finch: 'Texture poem for the moons of stars' from Typewriter Poems (1972), to Second Aeon and the author.

Ilse Garnier (as Pierre Garnier).

Pierre Garnier: Untitled from Prototypes (André Silvaire, 1964), to the author; 'Light' from Poèmes franco-japonais (André Silvaire, 1966), to Seiichi Niikuni and the author; 'Defeat of the Teutonic Knights at Tannenberg' from Text-Bilder (M. DuMont Schauberg, 1972), to the author; 'Vines' from Esquisses Palatines (André Silvaire, 1972), to the author; 'Vegetal sign' from An Anthology of Concrete Poetry (Something Else Press, 1967), to the author.

Michael Gibbs: 'In defence of poetry' from Connotations (1973), to Second Aeon and the author.

Tristan Gray Hulse: 'Moon song' and 'Moon loom', to the author.

Robin Greer: 'Buddhist mantra' from The Word as Image (Studio Vista, 1970), to the author.

Václav Havel: 'Estrangement' from Modulo, to the author.

Josef Hiršal: '4444', to the Stedelijk Museum and the author.

Will Hollis: 'Arab' and 'Police dog Tosca', to the British Typewriter Museum.

Josef Honys: 'Letter typogram', to the Stedelijk Museum.

Dom Sylvester Houédard: 'Sonic water' from The Word as Image (Studio Vista, 1970), to the author; 'Oracular stupor', 'Groovy for a good thing to happen' and two untitled red and blue typestracts, to the author; 'Italic ode', to Sandra Raphael and the author; 'Sardinian lovesong', to Nino Congiu and the author; untitled typestract from A, to the author.

Ernst Jandl: 'oeö' from Sprechblasen (Hermann Luchterhand, 1970), to the author.

Bengt Emil Johnson: 'Homage to John Cage' and untitled from Essaer om Bror Barsk och andra dikter (Albert Bonniers Förlag, 1964), to the author.

W. Bliem Kern: Two pages from Meditationsmeditationsmeditations (New Rivers Press, 1974), to the author.

Jiří Kolář: 'Albers' and 'Tinguely' from An Anthology of Concrete Poetry (Something Else Press, 1967), to the author; 'Fountain' from Text-Bilder (M. DuMont Schauberg, 1972), to the author; 'Brancusi' and two untitled, to the Stedelijk Museum and the author.

Richard Kostelanetz: 'Mullions' from Visual Language (Assembling Press, 1970), to the author.

Andrew Lloyd: '5th dolphin transmission' from Typewriter Poems (1972), to Second Aeon and the author.

Arrigo Lora-Totino: 'Space' from Concrete Poetry: a World View (Indiana University Press, 1968), to the author.

Steve McCaffery: Two panels from Carnival (Coach House Press, 1973), to the author.

Tim McDonough: 'Labyrinth', to the author.

Peter Mayer: Facet of the 'Yin Yang' cube, to the author.

Robert Morgan: 'Henri Chopin', to Tangent Records and the author.

Maurizio Nannucci: 'Black', 'White' and 'Yellow', to the author.

Seiichi Niikuni: 'Light' from Poèmes franco-japonais (André Silvaire, 1966), to Pierre Garnier and the author.

Simon Parritt: 'Grid 4' and 'Cityscape' from A, to the author.

Yüksel Pazarkaya: 'Guerilla' from Text-Bilder (M. DuMont Schauberg, 1972), to the author.

Zoran Popović: 'Portrait of the artist's wife' from Text-Bilder (M. DuMont Schauberg, 1972), to the author.

Alan Riddell: 'Homage to Vasarely', 'The honey pot' and 'Aubade' from Eclipse (1972) to Calder & Boyars and the author; 'Two flags' from London Magazine, to the author.

Toshihiko Shimizu: 'Six meditations', to the author.

Shohachirō Takahashi: 'Water land', to the author.

Stefan Themerson: 'Visual text', to Peter Mayer and the author.

Miroljub Todorović: 'Snake' from *Text-Bilder* (M. DuMont Schauberg, 1972), to the author.

Timm Ulrichs: 'Condensation' from *konkrete poesie* (Philip Reclam Jun., 1972) and 'Typotexture', to the author.

Jiří Valoch: Untitled, to the Stedelijk Museum and the author; and 'i' from *Concrete Poetry: a World View* (Indiana University Press, 1968), to the author.

J. P. Ward: 'Section through a tree-trunk' from *From Alphabet to Logos* (1972), to Second Aeon and the author.

H. N. Werkman: Typeprints on pages 19, 21, 22, 24, 25 and 26, to Groninger Museum; typeprints on pages 20 and 23, to Stedelijk Museum.

Emmett Williams: 'Like attracts like' and 'A festive marching song in the shape of 10 dixie cups' from *Concrete Poetry: an international anthology* (London Magazine Editions, 1967), to the author; and Prospectus for magazine Material, to the author.

Helmut Zenker: 'Sunday' from *Text-Bilder* (M. DuMont Schauberg, 1972), to the author.

Every effort has been made to trace the ownership of copyright material and make full acknowledgement for its use. Any information regarding omissions will be welcome.

Apart from thanking all the artists, poets and typographers without whose co-operation this book would not have been possible, I would like to thank particularly the following:

Alexander Moffatt, chairman of the New 57 Gallery Committee, Edinburgh, for in the first place encouraging my idea of an international exhibition of typewriter art and then showing it at the New 57 in November 1973; Richard Allen, Exhibition Consultant to the Polytechnic of Central London, for bringing the Edinburgh show to the Concourse Gallery, London, in February 1974; Liesbeth Crommelin, Assistant Curator, Department of Applied Art, Stedelijk Museum, Amsterdam, for lending a number of the Czechoslovak works for inclusion in the exhibitions and this book; J. van Loenen Martinet, Head of the Print Room, Stedelijk Museum, for lending six Werkman originals to the Edinburgh show; Mark Haworth-Booth, Assistant Keeper of Circulation, Victoria & Albert Museum, for lending the Tom Edmonds type tracks to the two shows and Miss Frances M. Newman and Dr Edmonds for allowing them to be in the book; W. A. Beeching, Director, British Typewriter Museum, Bournemouth, for lending the Will Hollis callitypes to the two shows and allowing them to be in the book; Derek Norman, for photographing many works for the original exhibition; Ian Barker, of the British Council, for facilitating the photographing of the Houédard typestracts; Allen Barker, for casting a painter's eye over the Introduction; A. G. H. Elsegood, of Pitman's, for unearthing Miss Stacey's butterfly from a mound of old numbers of the Phonetic Journal; lastly, Bob Cobbing and Peter Mayer, for helping so generously by lending books and for suggesting names for inclusion in the original exhibition.

Index by author

Index by country